CONTENTS

Acknowledgements   x

Contributors   xi

Preface   xii

Executive Summary   xv

PART 1 THE COST OF A CHILD

Chapter 1: Study Methodology   **1**
1   Introduction   2
1.1   The 'extra' cost of a child   3
1.2   The budget standard approach   4
1.3   The 'average' cost of a child   7
1.4   Summary   9

Chapter 2: Summary Findings   **11**
2.1   The cost of rearing a child   12
2.2   Comparisons with other studies   14
2.3   Raising children on an inadequate income   17
2.4   Child support entitlements in Ireland   18
2.5   Comparison with EU child income support schemes   23

Chapter 3: Policy Implications   **27**
3   Introduction   28
3.1   Reintroducing child tax allowances   28
3.2   Increasing child dependant allowances   28
3.3   Increasing child benefit   29
3.4   Policy recommendations   30
3.5   Summary   32

tro
lin

iii

PART 2 COSTING INDIVIDUAL EXPENDITURE CATEGORIES   **33**
Introduction   **34**

Chapter 4: Review of Family Budget Studies   **37**
4   Introduction   38
4.1   International family budget studies   38
4.2   Irish family budget studies   44

Chapter 5: Food   **47**
5   Introduction   48
5.1   Budgetary standards   48
5.2   Nutrition   50
5.3   Average food consumption   51
5.4   Dietary costings   52
5.5   Comparison of results   56
5.6   Summary   59

Chapter 6: Clothing   **61**
6   Introduction   62
6.1   Budgetary standards   62
6.2   Clothing requirements and lifespans   64
6.3   Clothing costs   66
6.4   Comparison of results   67
6.5   Summary   69

Chapter 7: Education and Extra-Curricular Costs   **71**
7   Introduction   72
7.1   Budgetary standards   73
7.2   Costing education: primary school costs   73
7.3   Costing education: post-primary school costs   77
7.4   Comparison of results   79
7.5   Summary   80

Chapter 8: Personal Care and Medical Costs   **81**
8   Introduction   82
8.1   Budgetary standards   82
8.2   Costing personal care and medical care   84
8.3   Comparison of results   89
8.4   Summary   90

Chapter 9: Housing   91
9   Introduction   92
9.1   Bedroom space   92
9.2   Tenure   92
9.3   Private rented housing   93
9.4   Local authority housing   93
9.5   Comparison of results   94
9.6   Summary   94

Chapter 10: Fuel   95
10   Introduction   96
10.1   Budgetary standards   96
10.2   Comparison of results   97
10.3   Summary   99

Chapter 11: Household Durables   101
11   Introduction   102
11.1   Budgetary standards   102
11.2   Costing household durables   102
11.3   Comparison of results   105
11.4   Summary   105

Chapter 12: Toys and Presents   107
12.   Introduction   108
12.1   Budgetary standards   108
12.2   Costing toys and presents   108
12.3   Summary   109

Chapter 13: Treats and Pocket Money   111
13.   Introduction   112
13.1   Budgetary standards   112
13.2   Comparison of results   114
13.3   Summary   114

Chapter 14: Outings and Holidays   115
14.   Introduction   116
14.1   Transport and outings   117
14.2   Holidays   117
14.3   Summary   119

Appendix A   **121**
Appendix B   **122**
Appendix C   **132**

Bibliography   **143**

LIST OF TABLES

Table   **Page**

1	Child Support in Ireland, Weekly Value, 1992	xx
2.1	Weekly Cost of a Child - Basic Minimum Standard, 1992	12
2.2	Weekly Additional Cost of a Modest-but-Adequate Standard	14
2.3	Weekly Cost of a Child (Conniffe & Keogh, 1992 Values)	15
2.4	The Relative Cost of a Child at Different Ages	16
2.5	Weekly Child Support Payments in Ireland, Full-Rates, 1992	19
2.6	Weekly Child Support Payments in Ireland, Full-Rates, 1993	20
5.1	Weekly Cost of Food - Basic Minimum Standard, 1992	49
5.2	Weekly Cost of food - Modest-but-Adequate Standard, 1992	49
5.3	Recommended Dietary Allowances by Age	50
5.4	Average Food Consumption of Children	53
5.5	Weekly Cost of Basic Diet, 1992	54
5.6	Basic Budget Standard for Food, Irish Prices 1992	56
5.7	Average Weekly Food Spending by Family Size, 1992	58
6.1	Comparison of Wardrobes for a Boy Aged 10-12	67
7.1	Annual Cost of Textbooks and Stationery, 1992	74
7.2	Annual Cost of Educating a Child at Primary Level, 1992	76
7.3	Annual Cost of Textbooks, Stationery and Equipment, 1992	77
7.4	Annual Cost of Educating a Child at Second Level, 1992	79
8.1	Itemised Weekly Cost of Personal Care - Basic Minimum Standard, 1992	83
8.2	Weekly Cost of Personal Care and Medical Care - Modest-but-Adequate, 1992	83
8.3	Cost of Nappies - Basic Minimum Standard, 1992	84
8.4	Cost of Baby Toiletries - Basic Minimum Standard, 1992	85
8.5	Cost of Toiletries - Basic Minimum Standard, 1992	86
8.6	Cost of Medical Care - Modest-but-Adequate Standard, 1992	88
10.1	Weekly Fuel Budgets for Children - Basic Minimum Standard, 1992	96
10.2	Clothes Washing by Family Size, 1992	97
10.3	Average Weekly Fuel Spending by Family Size	98
11.1	Spending on Household Durables - Basic Minimum Standard, 1992	102
11.2	Household Durables for 0-2 Year Olds - Basic Minimum Standard, 1992	103

11.3   Household Durables for 3-18 Year Olds
       - Basic Minimum Standard, 1992   104
12.1   Cost of a Selection of Toys   109
13.1   Weekly Cost of Pocket Money and Treats
       - Basic Minimum Budget Standard, 1992   113
13.2   Weekly Cost of Pocket Money and Treats
       - Modest-but-Adequate Standard, 1992   114

LIST OF FIGURES

Figure   Page

Figure		Page
1	Weekly Cost of a Child - Basic Minimum Standard, 1992	xviii
2	Weekly Cost of a Child - Modest-but-Adequate Standard, 1992	xix
2.1	Child Income Support Schemes for First Children in Europe, 1991	24
4	Average Weekly Cost of a Child	34
5.1	Weekly Cost of Food	48
5.2	Average Weekly Food Spending by Family Cycle, 1992	57
6.1	Weekly Cost of Clothes - Basic Minimum Standard, 1992	63
6.2	Average Weekly Spending on Children's Clothes by Family Cycle, 1992	68
7.1	Weekly Educational Costs for Primary and Secondary - Basic Minimum Standard, 1992	72
8.1	Weekly Cost of Personal Care - Basic Minimum Standard, 1992	82
9.1	Housing Tenure in Ireland	93
13.1	Weekly Cost of Pocket Money and Treats	112
14.1	Weekly Cost of Annual Holiday and Outings, 1992	116

ACKNOWLEDGEMENTS

This study on the financial cost of child-rearing in Ireland was commissioned by the Combat Poverty Agency and carried out by the Family Studies Centre, University College Dublin. The study was conducted by Claire Carney, Eithne Fitzgerald (until November 1992), Gabriel Kiely and Paul Quinn with the assistance of Evemarie Kimmerling. Evemarie's comprehensive review of the literature and methodology was invaluable to the research team. The research team would like to thank Mary Power for typing the final draft and for her invaluable editorial assistance. We are also grateful to Declan O'Donoghue and Trutz Haase, formerly of the Combat Poverty Agency, for their assistance and useful comments on earlier drafts, and to Helen Johnston and Niamh Flanagan, also of the Combat Poverty Agency, for bringing the report to publication.

The Family Studies Centre is an interdisciplinary centre concerned with promoting research on Irish families and contributing to and exploring the impact of social policy on the family.

CONTRIBUTORS

Claire Carney is an Honorary Senior Research Fellow in the Family Studies Centre at the National University of Ireland, University College Dublin and is currently engaged in research in Italy, Ireland and Portugal on behalf of the Council of Europe. She is the author of the book *Selectivity Issues in Irish Social Services*.

Eithne Fitzgerald is an economist and has worked as a freelance researcher on social policy issues. She was a member of the Commission on Social Welfare and her publications include the NESC report *Alternative Strategies for Family Income Support*. She was a member of the study team until her election to Dáil Éireann in November 1992.

Gabriel Kiely is Director of the Family Studies Centre, Dean of the Faculty of Philosophy and Sociology and Head of the Department of Social Policy and Social Work at the National University of Ireland, University College Dublin. He is a member of the European Union Observatory on National Family Policies.

Paul Quinn is a graduate of the University of Dublin, Trinity College where he studied economics and sociology. He has worked as a freelance researcher in the area of social and economic policy. His publications include *Energy and Equity*, a study of fuel poverty in the Tallaght area. He is presently working with the Work Research Co-operative, Economic and Social Consultants.

Evemarie Kimmerling is a graduate of the National University of Ireland, University College Dublin. She holds a Masters degree in social work from the University of Pittsburgh, where she specialised in poverty related issues and community development. She is presently working as a project manager with the ISPCC in a community based child and family centre.

PREFACE

The issue of child and family poverty is a key priority for the Combat Poverty Agency. Households with children, especially larger families, face a disproportionate risk of poverty in Ireland, and children are more likely to be in poverty than adults. These were two of the core findings resulting from the Survey of Income Distribution, Poverty and Usage of State Services carried out by the ESRI in 1987. Besides the alarming fact that poverty has been on the increase over the period 1973-1987, the survey found a substantial deterioration in the relative position of households with children. In percentage terms, the proportion of children in households falling below an income poverty line set at 50 per cent of average disposable household income increased by two-thirds from 16 per cent to 26 per cent over this period. It was in this context that the Combat Poverty Agency commissioned a study with the Family Studies Centre at University College Dublin to estimate the financial cost of child-rearing in Ireland and to compare these costings with existing child support measures.

The results presented in this report are disturbing. Child support payments provided by the State are falling short of even the minimal expenditure associated with the upbringing of a child. The study also demonstrates that the costs of rearing a child rise considerably with the age of the child and are about twice as high for teenagers as they are for younger children. Hence, while child support payments already fall short of the minimum costs during the early years of child-rearing, this shortfall becomes much greater in the teenage years.

The deterioration in the relative position of households with children has major implications for child income support policies. While there is no obligation *per se* for society to bear the whole costs associated with the upbringing of children, few would disagree that the state has at least some role to play in this respect. The Combat Poverty Agency believes society has an obligation to ensure that none of its members lives in poverty and that each of its citizens can afford minimum living standards which allow meaningful participation in economic, social and cultural life. This principle is widely acknowledged and put into practice by insuring against illness and by providing a pension after retirement from active working life. The child-rearing years similarly form a particular period of exceptional need within the life-cycle of a family and the same principle should be applied. The need for state support is particularly great in the case of children exposed to poverty through no fault of their own and who should enjoy the same chances as any other child. There is considerable evidence that children who grow up in poverty do less well educationally, suffer poorer health and have greatly reduced life chances. This cycle must be broken. The improvement in child support measures is not only imperative in the fight against child poverty but also constitutes a critical tool in the fight against poverty in general. As stated by Nolan (1993), the best child support policy mix should encompass the objectives of poverty alleviation, contribution to horizontal equity and the improvement of the position of women with dependant children without worsening of unemployment and poverty traps.

Since the publication of the initial ESRI/CPA report on poverty and the social welfare system in Ireland in 1988 the Government has introduced changes in the structure of family support measures. These changes were welcomed by the Combat Poverty Agency in so far as they represented a shift in the approach to family support. The rationalisation of child dependant allowances, the improvements in the Family Income Supplement scheme and the increased emphasis on child benefit are all steps in the right direction. However, as Nolan (1993) highlights many of these existing schemes of child support fall far short of achieving the best policy mix; for example child dependant allowances, while directing resources to those on low income, do not assist those in work on low incomes and contribute to the worsening of poverty traps. Improving Family Income Supplement, on the other hand, would ensure that those at work on low incomes were reached, but would produce high marginal tax benefit withdrawal rates and thus would further increase poverty traps. Nolan proposes increasing child benefit substantially, making it subject to income tax and reducing child dependant allowances by a proportion of the increase. The taxation of child benefit, endorsed by the Combat Poverty Agency, would provide the necessary revenue to increase the level of child benefit payment by about one-third. This scheme would ensure that all poor households with children were reached without restriction and without take-up problems. Moreover, poverty and unemployment traps would be avoided as payments would be received regardless of employment status.

While increased attention has been paid to the need for a fundamental reform in the structure of child support payments, the adequacy of current payments has received comparatively little attention. In this respect the present report is crucial. No previous studies in the Irish context have attempted to estimate the actual costs associated with rearing a child. With this information now available, which shows the gap between existing state support and even the minimum expenditures associated with rearing a child, there can be little doubt that the improvement of existing child support payments remains one of the most important tasks for Government in the immediate future.

In conclusion, two major lessons can be drawn from this report:
• First, the implementation of a sweeping reform of child benefit has to remain at the top of the political agenda. Child benefit payments should be increased substantially and made taxable in order to bring child support payments in line with the cost of rearing a child.
• Secondly, the study findings represent a strong case for the introduction of an age-related structure for child benefit which would take into account the significant rise in expenditure for older children.

Combat Poverty Agency
June 1994

THE COST OF A CHILD

Executive Summary

There are two kinds of costs associated with children: first, direct costs emanating from the purchase of food, clothing, education and similar areas of expenditure; and secondly, indirect costs such as the income foregone by parents providing full-time care, or the cost of substitute childcare where a parent works outside the home. This study focuses exclusively on the direct costs. In doing so it utilises what is called the budget standard approach, which gauges the cost of rearing a child in terms of a costed basket of goods and services. The selection of the items to be included in such a basket obviously has to take into account both what people actually buy as well as the minimal provisions necessary to satisfy the basic nutritional and other subsistence requirements of a child.

The budgets presented in this report have drawn on many sources: similar budget studies conducted in other countries, statistics on family expenditure in Ireland, studies of individual expenditure areas, and the research team's own knowledge and judgement. While not everyone may agree with the particular mix of goods and services provided in the two budget levels presented, the data collected for the study will allow readers to construct alternative estimates of appropriate budgets for children based on their own judgements as to children's basic needs.

The study team[1] was of the view that the cost of rearing a child includes not only subsistence expenditure such as food, clothes and shelter but also costs relating to a child's development and participation in the community, ie some modest spending on recreation and on toys and presents.

As there is no single objective or "right" way of establishing what should or should not be included in a consumption basket, the report provides estimates for the cost of rearing a child. Termed the **Basic Minimum Budget**, this standard provides for a basic diet, for a modest wardrobe, for basic schooling costs and for limited spending on recreation. Costs in this budget are kept to a minimum and many parents will choose to spend more on their children. Items excluded from the calculation are transport costs to school, medical costs and any increase in the overall housing costs (such as an extra bedroom). Also excluded are baby-sitting, childcare and pre-school education costs.

---

[1] The study team included Claire Carney, Eithne Fitzgerald, Gabriel Kiely, Paul Quinn and Eve Kimmerling.

There are many families who cannot afford the items included in this basic budget. These families survive by doing without. There is evidence that mothers in poor families are likely to be undernourished so that their children can be provided with basic nutritional requirements (see Lee and Gibney, 1989). Children in these families may have to wear second-hand or worn out clothing. Participation in out-of-school activities is another casualty of poverty, along with toys, presents and children's books. Family outings and holidays are a rarity in the poorest families. Lack of income can reinforce educational disadvantage where parents cannot afford books, outings or the cost of heating a separate room for study. Children in poverty lose out in terms of the norms of wider society, particularly in terms of opportunities to participate.

The fieldwork and pricing for this study was carried out in spring 1992. The average weekly cost of rearing children at the Basic Minimum Budget Standard is given in Figure 1 in three broad age groups at 1992 prices.

The main findings are: first, the costs associated with rearing a child to a basic minimum standard are £20-£40 per week, and secondly these costs differ considerably depending upon the age of the child. Costs are least for small children, amounting to about £20 per week, and rise to nearly twice that for teenage children.

A second estimate, provided for some commodity groups in the report, is called the **Modest-but-Adequate Budget Standard**. This cost estimate provides for a more varied diet, for some additional education expenses such as pre-school, one Gaeltacht holiday[2] and extra spending on toys and presents. On average, the additional costs to afford this standard amount to nearly £10 per week. Looking at the additional costs for each of the individual age bands, the Modest-but-Adequate Budget adds approximately one-quarter to the minimum cost estimates. Details of the additional costs for this second estimate are presented in Figure 2.

When these basic cost figures, in 1992 prices are compared with the level of support granted to families on social welfare in that year it is clear why

---

[2] "Gaeltacht" refers to the Irish speaking regions of Ireland. Summer schools are run in these regions to augment the Irish language studies of second level students. Participation in such "Gaeltacht holidays" has become relatively widespread in the past thirty years.

Figure 1 Weekly Cost of a Child - Basic Minimum Standard, 1992

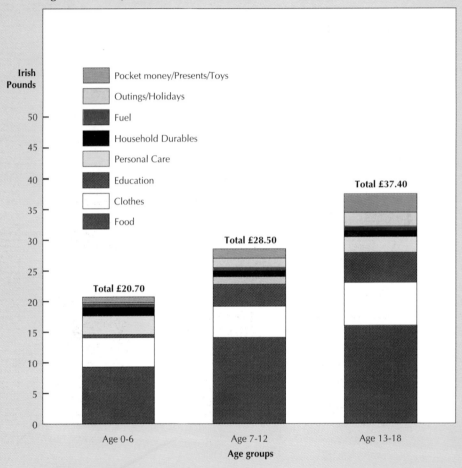

Source: Appendix C, Table C.1

child poverty has remained widespread in Ireland, (see Table 1). For most of those families in which neither parent had a job, the combined value of child benefit and child dependant allowances (CDAs) payable with welfare payments totalled £16.15 a week per child. The changes in rates of child benefit and of CDAs in 1993 brought this to £17.42 a week[3]. The totals are somewhat higher for fourth or later children in a family, and for the children of those on lone parent payments. Low income families in

Figure 2 Weekly Cost of a Child - Modest-but-Adequate Standard, 1992

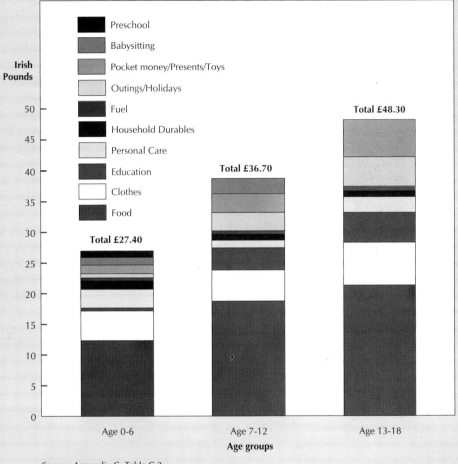

Source: Appendix C, Table C.2

employment may qualify for Family Income Supplement (FIS). In 1993 this was worth effectively £12 a week for each extra child in qualifying

---

[3] May 1994: In the 1994-95 budget the child benefit rate of £23 for fourth and subsequent children was increased to £25. The payment for third children was increased from £20 to £25 while the rate for first and second children remained at £20. Child dependent allowances were not changed. The new payments structure will be implemented in September 1994.

families, so that the level of combined child support to families on FIS was very similar to that available to families living on social welfare payments.

Only for the very youngest children do these combined child support payments approximate in any close way the cost of the Basic Minimum Budget costed in this report. For a twelve-year-old, official child support comes to roughly half of the estimated Basic Minimum Budget for this age group. The shortfall is even greater in respect of older teenagers who constitute the most expensive age group, causing major financial strain if these teenagers have no earnings of their own.

Obviously, there is an even wider gap between the levels of state child support and the higher level Modest-but-Adequate Budget.

Table 1 Child Support in Ireland, Weekly Value, 1992

Scheme	1st to 3rd Child		4th Child
	1992 £	1993 £	1992 and 1993 £
Child Benefit	3.65	4.61	5.30
Child Dependant Allowance	12.50	12.80	12.80
Total	**16.15**	**17.41**	**18.10**
Lone parents	**18.25**	**19.51**	**20.20**
Widows on contributory pensions	**19.85**	**21.11**	**21.80**

The importance of adequate child support payments becomes apparent in the context of children living in families dependent on social welfare. In 1992, some 350,000 children were living in families receiving the full-rate child dependant allowance (ie where either both parents were unemployed or where the family was headed by a single parent). Almost one-third of the children in Ireland were substantially dependent on state support for their upbringing. A further 100,000 children lived in families where one parent was unemployed and the other parent in paid employment (earning over £55 a week). About 26,700 children were in families receiving Family Income Supplement.

Without adequate child support payments, covering at least the most basic expenditure for the rearing of children, it would appear that child poverty is likely to remain a significant feature of the Irish economy for an indefinite period of time.

Part 1 of this report contains an overview of the methodology used in the study and a summary of the findings together with discussion of the main policy implications arising from these findings. Part 2 details more closely the composition and derivation of the selected commodity lists.

Chapter 1 - Study Methodology

1. Introduction

Not only is poverty in Ireland found disproportionately among larger families, but there has been a sustained deterioration in the economic situation of households with children over the past two decades (Nolan and Farrell, 1990). State child support, therefore, must constitute a major element in any anti-poverty strategy. It is vital that the level of child support to the poorest families should reflect the actual cost of bringing up children, particularly for families with a long-term dependence on social welfare. For this we need to know what it costs to rear a child.

Estimating the cost of bringing up children is important for many areas of public policy. The state shares with parents the cost of rearing the next generation through the provision of free and subsidised education, through the child benefit system, the provision of child allowances with social welfare payments, Family Income Supplement for parents in low-paid jobs, through tax exemptions awarded for children at the lowest income levels, and through the differentiation by means tests for state subsidised services according to family size. The courts, in cases of family breakdown, may also assess a share of the costs of rearing the children to be borne by each parent.

Despite this level of involvement, no official assessment of the costs of child-rearing informs these policies. The Commission on Social Welfare, for example, did present estimates of a basic cost of living for adults, but estimates in relation to children were not presented. The current study is an attempt to close this gap and ensure that policies and procedures relating to child support are adequately informed.

The basic aim of the study is to evaluate the cost of bringing up a child in Ireland, based on the budget standard approach, ie by pricing a basket of goods and services related to the prevailing norms of family living in Ireland today.

There are two kinds of costs associated with children: the direct costs associated with food, clothing, education and similar areas of expenditure; and, the indirect costs, for example the income forgone by a parent providing full-time care, or the cost of substitute childcare where a parent works outside the home. This study focuses exclusively on the direct costs of children. It excludes, therefore, any treatment of the income forgone when a parent works full-time in the home, or treatment of the childcare costs of working parents. These latter considerations are likely to make a much greater financial difference to parents of pre-school and younger children, and to be of less or no relevance in the teenage years.

1.1 The 'extra' cost of a child

This study attempts to estimate the extra costs which child-rearing brings to a family, by costing those items directly related to the child. It is fairly straightforward to attribute to a child the additional costs of his or her food, clothing, schooling and associated activities, personal care, toys, presents, treats and outings. It is a less straightforward task to separate the extra costs relating to children where parents and children consume goods in common, such as housing, fuel and light, household furnishings, or the use of the family car. In essence, we have attributed no extra costs to the household in respect of children for housing space, heating or the family car. Under fuel costs we have included extra costs for hot water, washing clothes, and lighting which can be attributed to each additional child. Estimates for the cost of outings and recreation include estimates of bus fare costs, but not for extra use of the family car. The cost of furnishing a child's bedroom, and the cost of baby equipment which is directly attributable to children have also been included, as well as the cost of seating and crockery for each child even though the latter represent a negligible amount. No figure is included for extra use or extra wear and tear on other household furniture, kitchen appliances or carpets. These issues are discussed in more detail in Part 2 of this report.

Substitution of spending patterns
There are many ways to estimate the cost of a child; the *1987 Household Budget Survey* for example, provides estimates of the cost of a child based on comparisons between the spending of households with children and those without children. This "extra spending" approach however, takes no account of spending choices. The distribution of the household budget will differ where parents substitute spending on their children for spending on themselves. In households without children, discretionary income may be spent on clothes, entertainment and holidays whereas families with children will tend to spend less discretionary income on adult items and more on their children. Therefore, the financial cost of a child to a family is likely to be more than the difference between what childless households and households with children spend.

The difference between the amounts which the adults in these two family types spend on themselves becomes clear when comparing the *Household*

3

Budget Survey figures for the spending patterns of couples with and without children (*1987 Household Budget Survey*, 1989, Table 8). In many cases parents make considerable sacrifices to ensure that their children have enough. Indeed, as Lee and Gibney's (1989) study of nutrition patterns among low-income families showed, some low-income parents are eating inadequate diets in order to provide their children with a balanced diet.

The current study, in costing the items directly related to the child, does not attempt to estimate the extent of this substitution effect. Instead, a different method is adopted whereby the marginal cost of a child is estimated using the budget standard approach. However, where possible, comparisons have been made with *Household Budget Survey* data, bearing in mind the limitations of these data for direct comparative purposes.

1.2 The budget standard approach

Different approaches have been used in the literature to measure the cost of rearing children (for a review, see Part 2 of this report; Conniffe and Keogh, 1988:5-8; Oldfield, 1993: 1-5). The most straightforward approach is to make a list of what a child needs with regard to food, clothing and other basic requirements, and then to establish how much this will cost. This involves making normative judgments based on "expert" opinions of a child's needs. Lists of goods and services can be drawn up to meet a variety of living standards, from subsistence through modest-but-adequate to generous. This approach is prescriptive, in the sense that it sets out what is deemed to be necessary and thus what ought to be spent in order to live at one of these living standards. The judgements of what to include in a basic budget are critical. It is possible, for example, to cost a budget around a nutritionally adequate diet which bears little relation to the food that families actually buy and consume.

A second approach, the behavioural approach, looks at what is actually spent on goods and services. Principally, this method involves surveying groups of people to determine what is actually spent and using econometric techniques to capture variations in expenditure according to family composition. The danger of an analysis undertaken purely on the basis of actual behaviour is that, at lower levels of income, it could produce a cost norm which does not in fact secure an acceptable minimum living standard. In particular, it could result in a food basket which does not provide for the minimum nutritional requirements of a child.

4

To overcome the shortcomings of the above mentioned methods, this study utilises the budget standard approach. This approach attempts to combine both absolute and relative concepts of need. It uses expenditure surveys to inform its choice of which areas of expenditure to include. This method combines both an assessment of physical needs and of social norms. The problem of how accurate it is possible to be in determining what to include in a budget standard has been discussed by Piachaud (1984:152) and Bradshaw *et al* (1987:169). Piachaud argues that, while a definition of what is needed for adults may be problematic, "for some groups there may be a reasonable degree of social consensus. For children a user-friendly diet, clothing, heating, toys, school outings and a holiday, are probably viewed as necessities by most" (1984:152).

Estimating the cost of a child can vary considerably according to the kind of living standard which is taken as the basis of the cost estimate. This cost can be estimated at any one of a variety of living standards from basic minimum, to modest-but-adequate, to prevailing, to generous. In this respect it is interesting to observe that in recent British research into poverty and deprivation the emphasis has shifted from physical requirements for mere survival to the principle of a minimum amount of resources required to lead a normal life (see for example Townsend, 1979; Mack and Lansley, 1985). On similar reasoning, the study group has included costs associated with participation in society, along with the costs of such items as food and clothing in the belief that all of the costs involved in these budgets reflect the realistic needs of children. Nevertheless, the reader should be aware that they are ultimately based on normative judgements.

Review of family budget studies
The current study uses the budget standard method - a costed basket of goods and services whose selection reflects actual expenditure data. To this end, a number of Irish and international studies of family budgets were examined to select items for inclusion and to assess the average lifespans of any item included (see Part 2, Appendix B). Of particular help in this respect was the detailed work of the Family Budget Unit at the University of York, which drew on expert teams under each commodity heading. Differences in styles of living, climatic conditions, and housing tenure made the use of budget studies from other countries less straightforward. In addition, in order to sound out tentatively the validity of the study team's choice of consumer goods, a wide range of expenditure relating to children was

5

discussed with two panels of mothers, one in a low-income Dublin suburb and one in a rural area in the west of Ireland.

The terms of reference used in this study required the study group to look at the cost of *individual children* in a family. In contrast, many international studies look at the cost of *families* of varying composition rather than the cost of individual children; thus direct comparisons were difficult to make. Moreover, while this study deals with an age range which runs from babyhood to age eighteen, most international studies deal with children in a very restricted range of age groups - the Family Budget Unit in York for example, looked only at a boy aged ten and a girl aged four (1990). These other studies afforded only minimal guidance to the study team in costing budgets for children in other age groups. Where no comparable budget studies were available for the particular age categories addressed, the estimates presented reflect the judgement of the study team alone.

Two different levels of budget standards for children are estimated in the report. The first, termed the Basic Minimum Budget, is based on a minimum cost but nutritionally adequate diet, a modest clothing budget, schooling costs, recreation, pocket money and very basic spending on outings, holidays and presents. This budget only allows for a basic minimum participation in recreation and local activities.

The second budget, which is termed the Modest-but-Adequate Budget, covers additional items in some commodity groups: a more varied diet, attendance at pre-school, baby-sitting costs, a Gaeltacht holiday[4] at age fifteen, a fortnight's summer holiday instead of the five days included in the Basic Minimum budget, and extra spending on toys and presents.

Whether the list of goods and services included in the consumption bundles are reasonably representative, and whether their prices and expected lifespans are shown realistically, has ultimately to be judged by the readers themselves. However, the detailed listing in Part 2 of this report makes it

---

[4] "Gaeltacht" refers to the Irish speaking regions of Ireland. Summer schools are run in these regions to augment the Irish language studies of second level students. Participation in such "Gaeltacht holidays" has become relatively widespread in the past thirty years.

possible for anyone to make any adjustments considered necessary. Finally, when interpreting the budgets presented in this report, the reader should be aware of how these estimates have been arrived at. The procedure used is outlined in detail in Part 2 of this report.

1.3 The 'average' cost of a child

The estimates presented in this report are attempts to construct average budgets, that is to say they do not take into account the variations that exist from family to family in the spending choices made, or the variations from child to child in terms of preferences and pastimes. Some of these may balance each other out - what one family spends on football for example, another may spend on visits to the cinema.

In pricing a particular basket of goods and services at each age level, the ways in which the composition of the basket may change depending on the composition of the household have not been taken into account. The two levels of budget, the Basic Minimum and the Modest-but-Adequate, are the only variations in spending provided for in response to variations in the levels of income per head. However, larger families with less income per head may buy different foods than smaller families with the same income. The same menus are assumed to operate at different family sizes. Neither do the totals include the extra costs involved where a child has a particular medical condition or illness, although there clearly will be particular circumstances where the cost of maintaining a child will exceed the estimates for such reasons.

Rural/urban differences

A number of divergences exist in spending habits and lifestyle patterns between rural and urban households as shown for example in the *1987 Household Budget Survey*. Differences in urban and rural spending patterns were also reflected in the discussions conducted with the panels of mothers. In rural areas, school transport could impose a significant cost in respect of children not eligible for free transport. Because school children in rural areas spend so much time in travel, there was less opportunity, and hence less expense, in relation to after-school activities. School holidays also appeared to be more expensive for parents in urban areas, because in rural areas a greater range of activities were available in summer at little or no extra cost.

Heating costs also proved likely to vary between urban and rural areas. Most families on the discussion panel who were living in rural areas were living in houses heated with solid fuel central heating. In contrast, most of the families on the urban panel were using open fires as their primary source of heating and many were paying for hot water separately. Since however, heating as a household overhead has not been taken in this study to be related to the number of children in a family, this element of urban/rural difference would be likely to have little bearing on the estimates as a whole.

Pricing

The fieldwork and pricing for the study was carried out in spring 1992, mainly using local branches of national chainstores. Part 2 of this report details the way in which individual items were priced. In relation to school costs, prices in Dublin schools were compared with the National Parents Council studies (1990 and 1991) of a Tipperary school in an attempt to keep urban/rural, or regional variations in prices at a minimum.

Average weekly costs

There are obvious seasonal variations in spending on clothing, fuel, back to school needs, and at Christmas time. In deriving an estimated weekly cost of child-rearing, the approach in the current study has been to average spending on seasonal items over the entire year. Similarly, for less frequent purchases such as furniture or clothing, an average weekly cost is derived by estimating a lifespan for each of these items. The estimates of the average weekly cost of less-frequently-bought items are obviously particularly sensitive to the estimated lifespans. Where possible these estimates have been based on those available from similar studies. In the case of clothes there is a clear relationship between the items possessed and the speed at which they wear out. For example, one jumper will last longer if it is worn every second day rather than being worn every day.

Economies of scale

One important question which needs to be addressed is whether families may benefit from economies of scale, in other words, whether the cost of rearing a child in a larger family is any cheaper than in a smaller family. The limitations of this study did not allow any conclusions to be reached in regard to such economies of scale. Areas where economies of scale may be apparent are discussed in more detail in Chapter 2. Jointly consumed goods such as housing, TV and heating were excluded from the budgets presented, so that their contribution to economies of scale is not captured. A second saving occurring in larger families is where goods can be passed down from one child to another. Estimates, for example, of savings on baby equipment for later children are presented in the report. The scope for passing on clothes from one child to another depends on the ages of children and on their relative size, shape and gender. Passing on clothes is probably most practical for babies and younger children. A third possible source of economies of scale is where savings can be made on bulk purchasing, for example of food, or where the purchase of double-sized furniture amounts to less than twice the cost of an item for one person. No allowance has been made in this study for this potential source of economies; however one would expect such savings to be of relatively minor significance.

Conniffe and Keogh (1988) in their study of equivalence scales found economies of scale to be occurring as a result of an increase in family size. Their study was confined to only one- and two-child families, and to children aged under five and aged between five and fourteen. Economies of scale, they found, were much more pronounced in the case of children under five than those in the five to fourteen age-group. Conniffe and Keogh's estimates suggested (subject to sampling error) that spending on clothes for a family with two children aged under five represents the same cost as for a family with one child aged under five. Household overheads, such as heating and transport, for which no cost has been attributed in the current study, are the other main potential sources of economies of scale noted by Conniffe and Keogh.

1.4 Summary

This section has introduced and described the budget standard method used in this study, comparing it with other potential approaches. Areas of expenditure included in the current study are food, clothes, education and extra-curricular activities, personal care, household durables and fuel costs to the extent that they can be directly attributed to the child, pocket money, outings, holidays, presents and toys. Expenditures where the child shares the use of a common household good are excluded from the cost estimates. These are of particularly relevance to any share in the cost of housing and general heating. Finally, any "opportunity costs" arising for families as a result of having children are excluded, for example the potential income forgone by any parent not working outside the home. In the next chapter, the aggregate outcomes which emerged from the study, are examined.

Chapter 2 - Summary Findings

2.1 The cost of rearing a child

This report presents two estimates of the direct individual cost of rearing a child in Ireland: (i) a Basic Minimum Budget Standard which provides for a basic diet, a modest wardrobe, essential schooling costs and limited spending on recreation, outings, holidays and presents; and (ii) a Modest-but-Adequate Budget Standard which provides for a more varied diet, for additional spending on toys and presents, and for extra educational expenditure such as pre-school participation and a visit to the Gaeltacht.

Both budgets include spending which can be directly attributed to the child and exclude costs shared in common with parents such as housing, heating, household furniture and equipment (other than furnishings for the child's room) as well as usage of the family car. The Basic Minimum Budget, the main focus of the study, excludes medical costs (a medical card is assumed at this income level), and baby-sitting costs. Allowance is made, however, for pocket-money and for very basic spending on recreation, outings, holidays and presents, since it was considered that such leisure activity costs would be likely to weigh heavily on low-income families. The resulting estimates of average weekly costs for children of different ages are shown in Table 2.1. These estimates represent an aggregation of costs for boys and girls. Gender differences in costs are discussed under the relevant commodity groups in Part 2 of the report.

Table 2.1 Weekly Cost of a Child - Basic Minimum Standard, 1992

Age/ Item	under1 £	1-2 £	3-4 £	5-6 £	7-8 £	9-10 £	11-12 £	13-14 £	15-16 £	17-18 £
Food	5.80	8.81	8.81	11.84	13.26	13.26	15.58	15.58	16.13	16.13
Clothes	5.55	5.46	4.10	4.46	5.08	5.08	5.08	7.02	7.02	7.02
Education	-	-	-	1.70	2.82	3.84	4.14	5.24	5.94	3.40
Personal care	7.64	4.43	1.24	1.24	1.24	1.24	1.24	2.55	2.55	2.62
Household Durables	1.86	1.86	0.94	0.94	0.94	0.94	0.94	0.94	0.94	0.94
Fuel	0.56	0.56	0.56	0.56	0.56	0.56	0.56	0.80	0.80	0.80
Outings and Holiday	-	-	-	0.83	1.33	1.33	1.83	1.92	1.92	2.92
Pocket money, Toys and Presents	0.77	0.77	0.97	1.17	1.34	1.34	1.90	2.47	3.04	3.61
Totals*	**22.20**	**21.90**	**16.60**	**22.70**	**26.60**	**27.60**	**31.30**	**36.50**	**38.30**	**37.40**

* rounded to the nearest 10p

The average costs associated with rearing a child under this budget amount to about £30 per week. These costs, however, differ considerably depending on the age of the child. During the early years of childhood costs fall slightly, reaching their lowest level of £17 per week at age four. After this, costs increase rapidly, reaching a maximum of £38 per week for children in their late teens. If one divides the time over which parents provide for their children into three equal intervals of six years each, the costs average roughly £20, £30 and £40 per week for the first, second and third periods respectively.

Looking at the individual cost components, food is by far the largest contributor to the overall cost of rearing a child. With the exception of infants under one year of age, whose food accounts for just over one-quarter (26%) of total expenditure, in all other age groups food makes up the largest proportion (40-53%) of the total cost. Clothes and education are the next most important expenditure items for all groups.

Table 2.2 shows the additional expenditure occurring when applying a Modest-but-Adequate Budget Standard. Primarily, this includes a more varied diet, adding between £1.93 and £5.38 extra per child per week. Also included in this estimate are: a fortnight's holiday instead of the five days allowed for in the Basic Minimum Budget; a doubling of the budget for pocket money, toys and presents; an allowance for pre-school cost at age three to four; and £2.50 in baby-sitting costs for children between the ages of three years and twelve years to allow their parents one night out every fortnight. Affording a Modest-but-Adequate Budget Standard in rearing a child, adds about £2.70 weekly to the basic minimum costs in the youngest age group, and about £11.20 where children are fifteen years and older. Thus, the total cost of a child at a Modest-but-Adequate Budget Standard also rises steadily depending on the age of the child and amounts to £24.90 per week for those in the youngest age group and £49.15 per week for those aged fifteen years upwards.

Table 2.2 Weekly Additional Cost of a Modest-but-Adequate Standard

Age/ Item	under1 £	1-2 £	3-4 £	5-6 £	7-8 £	9-10 £	11-12 £	13-14 £	15-16 £	17-18 £
Food	1.93	2.94	2.94	3.95	4.42	4.42	5.19	5.19	5.38	5.38
Outings/Holidays	-	-	-	1.49	1.49	1.49	1.49	2.53	2.53	2.53
Pocket money, toys and presents	0.77	0.77	0.97	1.17	1.34	1.34	1.90	2.47	3.04	3.61
Baby-sitting	-	-	2.50	2.50	2.50	2.50	2.50	-	-	-
Pre-school	-	-	4.15	-	-	-	-	-	-	-
Total extra costs	**2.70**	**3.71**	**10.56**	**9.11**	**9.75**	**9.75**	**11.08**	**10.19**	**10.95**	**11.52**
Total Costs for Modest-but-Adequate Standard*	**24.90**	**25.60**	**27.20**	**31.90**	**36.30**	**37.30**	**42.40**	**46.70**	**49.30**	**49.00**

* rounded to the nearest 10p

2.2 Comparisons with other studies

Conniffe and Keogh (1988)

To date, the most important Irish study on the cost of a child is that of Conniffe and Keogh (1988). Although Conniffe and Keogh based their analysis on the *1980 Household Budget Survey*, they also provided a method by which one could update and extrapolate results for future years, which makes their findings still worthwhile as a comparison. Their approach is briefly described before citing their results.

Conniffe and Keogh estimate the extra costs arising in certain households *with children* compared to a reference household type that is alike in all other respects but without children. The household types included in their analysis consist of two adults and one or two children below fifteen years of age, and they distinguish between the ages of children under and over five years of age. Thus households with dependent children aged over fifteen years are excluded from the study, as are single parent households, households with adult dependants and households of various other compositions.

Their method, using the linear expenditure system, separates spending into a basic component and an element which varies with income, which they termed *discretionary expenditure*. Their basic cost estimates can therefore be compared with the Basic Minimum Budget Standard which has been estimated for this report using an entirely different method. Table 2.3 below, shows Conniffe and Keogh's estimates for the cost of a child, updated to 1992 values.

Table 2.3 Weekly Cost of a Child, (Conniffe and Keogh, 1992 values)

Household Composition/ Item	1 child Under 5 £	1 child aged 5-15 £	2 children under 5 £	2 children aged 5-15 £	1 child under 5 &1 child aged 5-15 £
Food	4.61	10.38	9.23	20.76	14.99
Clothing & Footwear	1.80	1.80	1.80	4.09	1.80
Fuel & Light	1.05	1.05	1.75	1.75	1.75
Durables	0.68	0.68	0.68	0.68	0.68
Other Goods	2.81	2.16	2.81	2.81	2.81
Transport	11.53	11.53	11.53	11.53	11.53
Services	0.00	4.82	0.00	9.38	4.82
Total	**22.49**	**32.42**	**27.80**	**51.00**	**38.38**

Source: Conniffe and Keogh, 1988;
Prices extrapolated to 1992 values using commodity price index for August of respective years.

Comparing the total cost of a child in households consisting of two adults and one child (ie the first two columns in Table 2.3) Conniffe and Keogh's findings are remarkably similar to the estimates of the Basic Minimum Budget Standard in the current study. Furthermore, they not only coincide in the actual level, but also display the same increase as the child grows older. However, Conniffe and Keogh differ considerably from the current study in their estimates of the individual expenditure components. In particular, their estimates (which are subject to sampling error) for the transport component appear very large for smaller families, and it is counter-intuitive that transport costs would be double the cost of food even for a toddler, and would account for half the cost of a child in the "one child under five" category. It is also notable that they derive lower food costs. Due to the relatively lesser importance attributed to the food component, and the inclusion of certain household overheads not attributed to children in the current study, Conniffe and Keogh assign greater importance to economies of scale.

McClements (1978)

The current study's finding that costs rise with the age of a child is not surprising and has been substantiated by many other studies. McClements (1978), in his study of equivalence scales[5] using the UK Family Expenditure Survey, shows a very clear relationship between the cost of a child and the age of a child. McClements's findings remain the basis which underpin the UK child support system and it is interesting to note in this context, that the UK child support system has, from its inception after World War II, always acknowledged the greater costs of older children.

McClements's results, and the findings of this study, show a strong degree of similarity in the pattern of the cost of children at different ages. His figures relate the cost of children of different ages to a reference household of a married couple without children. His method, and the method used in this study, are different; the method used in this study being a costed basket of goods and services, his being an econometric analysis of variations in actual household spending related to family size. Unlike Conniffe and Keogh, McClements's analysis assumes that the cost of children is proportional to family income at all levels.

Table 2.4 The Relative Cost of a Child at Different Ages

Age	McClements	The Current Study
0-under 1	.09	.17
2-4	.18	.13
5-7	.21	.18
8-10	.23	.22
11-12	.25	.25
13-15	.27	.29
16-18	.36	.30

[5] To limit the effect of variations in household composition and associated factors equivalence scales are used. Equivalence scales apply a system of weighting to household members to bring total household income to a common base thus permitting valid comparisons to be made between households of differing composition.

2.3 Raising children on an inadequate income

For most parents on social welfare in Ireland, current child support payments are significantly lower than the Basic Minimum Budget Standard presented in this study. Indeed, for children aged over twelve years who live in families dependent on social welfare, the support granted by the state to their parent(s) amounts to little more than half the cost of rearing that child to the standard set in this basic budget. For many families on social welfare, but particularly for those headed by a single parent or with one parent claiming long-term unemployment assistance, social welfare may remain their sole source of income for many years. These families can only manage by cutting back on their own living standard and that of their children, otherwise bills, debts and borrowing can set up a vicious circle from which it can be difficult to escape.

Food expenditure amounts to roughly half the total cost of the Basic Minimum Budget Standard. The shortfall between state child support payments and this estimated budget cost means that some items essential to maintain a nutritionally adequate diet may have to be omitted. Lee and Gibney (1989) suggest that it may often be the parents who eat less adequately in these circumstances to ensure their children have sufficient food.

Clothing is another area where significant shortfalls from the basic clothing standard are likely to occur. It is estimated in the current study that the cost of a basic school outfit priced in a chainstore, consisting of one pair of school trousers, a jumper, two shirts, a new pair of shoes and a winter anorak, would amount to £53 for a five to six year old and £100 for a teenager. Underwear and socks would incur additional expenditure. In 1993 the Back-to-School Clothing and Footwear Allowance at £35 for primary students and £50 for second level students is clearly, as other studies have shown, inadequate to meet the expense of basic school clothes. In her analysis of expenditure data from the *1987 Household Budget Survey*, Murphy-Lawless (1992) found that a family on social welfare with two children spends only a quarter as much on clothes as a comparable family on average income. Such a low level of expenditure can only be sustained by expecting clothes to last well beyond their normal lifespans and by using second-hand articles.

The free schoolbooks scheme has also been shown to be underfunded: "Needy" pupils, identified by school principals, are paid £5.50 toward the cost of schoolbooks in junior infant cycle and £10 in higher primary classes.

Schoolbooks are estimated to cost £23 in junior infant cycle, about £54 in sixth class (although there could be some scope at this level for passing on books), and £60-£140 at secondary level, depending on the class. While a per pupil rate for secondary students is not set, in 1992 the average payment per pupil was £24.52. In relation to other school-going costs, only a minority of children are eligible for free school meals (the free school meals scheme is discussed in greater detail below).

Fuel bills can present a major worry for families depending on social welfare, so much so that heating an extra room for study will often be out of the question. Participation in extra-curricular activities, such as outings and holidays is likely to prove another casualty even though such participation constitutes an essential element of a child's healthy development. The St. Vincent de Paul Society reported in its submission to the Commission on Social Welfare (Table 5.4, 1986) that almost 90 per cent of a sample of 800 families which its members were visiting had no holiday in two years and that 70 per cent of these families had not had an outing together in two years. Mothers interviewed for the current study expressed the heartbreak they experienced in asking their children to forgo or to abandon activities like dancing or taking music lessons because they could not afford the cost. They also spoke of the difficulties of trying to keep children amused over the long summer break without sufficient money.

2.4 Child support entitlements in Ireland

The most widespread, though not necessarily the most significant form of child income support in Ireland, is child benefit. Child benefit is a universal payment, paid by the state for all children up to age sixteen, and for those in full-time education up to age eighteen. In addition to this, parents on social welfare payments are eligible for additional child dependant allowances. Child dependant allowances are paid at the full rate where both parents are out of work and at half rate where one parent earns over £55 per week (£60 per week from 1993[6]). Some 350,000 children live in families where the full rate child dependant allowance is paid. Up to a third of all children in the state are living in families wholly or mainly dependent on weekly social welfare payments. A further 100,000 children live in families with one parent on welfare while the other is in employment.

---

[6] This income threshold remained unchanged at £60 in the 1994-95 budget.

Table 2.5 Weekly Child Support Payments in Ireland, Full-Rates 1992

Scheme	1st Child £	2nd Child £	3rd Child £	4th & later Child £
Child Benefit	3.65	3.65	3.65	5.30
Child Dependant Allowance	12.50	12.50	12.50	12.50
Total	**16.15**	**16.15**	**16.15**	**17.80**
Old-Age Contributory Pension	+2.10	+2.10	-	-
Invalidity Pension	+2.10	+2.10	-	-
Lone Parent's Allowance	+2.10	+2.10	+2.10	+2.10
Widow's Contributory Pension	+3.70	+3.70	+3.70	+3.70
Deserted Wife's Benefit	+3.70	+3.70	+3.70	+3.70
Back to School, Primary level*	+0.70	+0.70	+0.70	+0.70
Back to School, Second level*	+1.00	+1.00	+1.00	+1.00

* shown as weekly equivalent
Source: Department of Social Welfare, 1992

At the time that this study was undertaken (ie 1992) the combined income support from child benefit and child dependant allowances amounted to £16.15 per week for most parents on welfare for each of the first three children, and to £17.80 per week for fourth and subsequent children. In September 1993, child benefit was increased to £20 a month for the first three children, and to £23 a month for fourth and later children. Child dependant allowances also increased from £12.50 to £12.80 per week giving a combined support of £17.40 per week for the first three children and £18.11 per week for fourth and subsequent children[7]. Child support payments are slightly higher (£18.25 in 1992, and £18.55 in 1993) for families where a parent claims an Old-Age Contributory Pension or an Invalidity

---

[7] May 1994: In the 1994-95 budget the child benefit rate of £23 for fourth and subsequent children was increased to £25. The payment for third children was increased from £20 to £25 while the rate for first and second children remained at £20. Child dependant allowances remain unchanged. The new payments structure will be implemented in September 1994.

19

Pension or Lone Parent's Allowance[8]. Where a parent receives the Widow's Contributory Pension or the Deserted Wife's Benefit, the combined child support payments came to £19.85 (1992) and to £21.10 (1993) per week[9]. Table 2.6 below summarises the main payments made in support of children in 1993.

Table 2.6 Weekly Child Support Payments in Ireland, Full-Rates 1993

Scheme	1st Child £	2nd Child £	3rd Child £	4th & later Child £
Child Benefit	4.60	4.60	4.60	5.30
Child Dependent Allowance	12.80	12.80	12.80	12.80
Total	**17.40**	**17.40**	**17.40**	**18.10**
Old-Age Contributory Pension	+ 2.10	+ 2.10	-	-
Invalidity Pension	+ 2.10	+ 2.10	-	-
Lone Parent's Allowance	+ 2.10	+ 2.10	+ 2.10	+ 2.10
Widow's Contributory Pension	+ 3.70	+ 3.70	+ 3.70	+ 3.70
Deserted Wife's Benefit	+ 3.70	+ 3.70	+ 3.70	+ 3.70
Back to School, Primary level*	+ 0.70	+ 0.70	+ 0.70	+ 0.70
Back to School, Second level*	+ 1.00	+ 1.00	+ 1.00	+ 1.00

* shown as weekly equivalent
Source: Department of Social Welfare, 1993

In addition to this, 7,700 families with 26,700 child dependants receive Family Income Supplement (FIS). FIS is means-tested and is paid where a parent works full-time (a minimum of twenty hours per week) but where the average weekly family income remains below a certain figure, depending upon the relative family size. This figure rises in stages of £20 per week for each child. The supplement is then assessed at 60 per cent of the difference

[8] Child dependant allowances paid to parents on the Old-Age Contributory Pension, Invalidity Pension and Lone Parent's Allowance were increased to £15.20 in the 1994 budget giving a combined child support payment of £19.82.
[9] Child dependent allowances paid to parents in receipt of the Widow's Contributory Pension or the Deserted Wife's Benefit were increased to £17.00 in 1994 giving a combined child support payment of £21.60.

between the actual weekly family income and the fixed amount for family size. The imputed support for children of £12 (60 per cent of £20) is hence analogous to the level of support afforded by the state to most parents in receipt of the full-rate child dependant allowances.

Social welfare recipients, including those employed under a Social Employment Scheme (SES) or attending a FAS training course, may also be eligible to receive a Back-to-School Clothing and Footwear Allowance for each school-going child at the start of the school year[10]. This allowance currently stands at £35.00 for primary school children and at £50.00 for second level children or 70p and £1 per week respectively. A small number of parents are also eligible to receive assistance with the cost of schoolbooks, and their children eligible to receive free school meals[11] in urban areas and in certain areas of the Gaeltacht.

The structure of child support in Ireland
Unlike the UK, child support payments in Ireland are not age-related, yet estimates in this report suggest that the cost of rearing a child rises steadily with the increasing age of the child. Food, for example, accounts for roughly half the total cost of a child This is directly related to the age and energy needs of growing children. Once past the pre-school stage, it is likely that more food will be consumed and clothing more frequently replaced. Costs associated with transport and recreation are also positively correlated with age. The onset of puberty and the transition to second-level school at around age twelve mark a particular turning point in a child's development. This stage of development is associated with a distinct shift in costs; for example, older children in general will be likely to incur higher levels of social and recreational expenditure than younger children.

The position of a child in the family also appears to affect the cost of the child; second children may cost up to £3 less per week if clothing,

---

[10] In addition to the SES, the Community Employment Development Programme (CEDP) was introduced in October 1992. These schemes will be replaced by the Community Employment Scheme (CES) in late 1994. Recipients on the CEDP and CES retained their eligibility for the Back-to-School Clothing and Footwear Allowance for each school-going child.

[11] In 1992, 369 schools participated in the free school meals scheme with 71,377 children benefiting. Free school meals usually constitute a snack of milk and a bun, not a full meal.

schoolbooks and equipment can be handed on by older siblings. However, despite such apparent economies of scale, families with higher numbers of children are overrepresented in poverty statistics. Calculations based on data published by the Department of Social Welfare (1990 and 1991a) show that, of the estimated 49,000 fifth or later children in Irish families in 1990, 20,000 were living in families living on social welfare payments as were half of all families with six or more children. In their analysis of the *ESRI Survey of Income Distribution, Poverty and Usage of State Services*, Callan *et al* (1989) equally showed the prevalence of poverty among families with children: whereas only 15 per cent of couple-only households were below the poverty line in 1987, this figure rose to 29 per cent in the case of lone parents and to 36 per cent in the case of families with four or more children. While this evidence is undisputed, the extent of the current study did not enable an assessment as to whether costs were greater for larger families.

Child benefit payments are higher in Ireland for fourth and subsequent children[12]. There are also larger income tax exemption limits for low-income families as the family size increases[13]. Means tests for various benefits, from Family Income Supplement to medical cards to higher education grants, are graduated by family size, and in each case there is an implicit cost allowed for each extra child.

Recent studies have shown that lone parent families in Ireland form a significant and growing proportion of families living in poor economic circumstances (Callan *et al*, 1989). In accordance with this situation, child dependant allowances for lone parents are higher in Ireland than for married or cohabiting parents. It is difficult to establish, however, whether single parents experience higher child-rearing costs than married or cohabiting parents (see Department of Social Welfare, 1991b). It is therefore interesting to note that Carroll, J, in *MacMathuna v Ireland and the Attorney General*, 1990, in the High Court held that the payment of a more generous allowance to an unmarried than to a married mother was justified

---

[12] In the 1994-95 budget Child Benefit payments for third and subsequent children were brought on a par with payments for fourth and subsequent children.
[13] Child additions to the low-income exemption limits in 1992 were £300 for first and second children and £500 for third and subsequent children. These were increased to £350 and £550 respectively in 1993 and again to £450 and £650 in 1994.

on grounds of the burden of parenthood falling more heavily upon the single parent.

Since child dependant allowances form the mainstay of child support payments provided by the state and are available only to parents out of work, families where the parents are in paid employment receive only a fraction of the cost of child-rearing. This system of child support can create disincentives for parents to take up employment, particularly amongst larger families. The level of wages is also an important consideration for parents of large families in the decision to take up work. While this may have little effect on the overall level of unemployment, it clearly must affect the composition of those who are unemployed and contribute to the growing segregation in the labour market. Indeed, in 45 per cent of families with four or more children, neither of the parents are in employment. As a consequence, a substantial proportion of the next generation is being reared in families with both parents frequently or permanently out of work.

2.5 Comparison with EU child income support schemes

Historically, child income support was conceived as a measure to enable families cope more adequately with the economic burden children represent. At present, three models exist in the EU for this purpose. One is a universal system; the second is based on income and therefore means-tested; and the third is one that pays a universal benefit to all and allocates an additional supplementary higher amount to lower income groups. In addition, child income support can be social security based or tax based. Where it is social security based, the amounts payable can vary according to different entitlements under the social security system. Where it is tax based, this variation does not exist.

Greece, Italy and Spain are the only EU countries in which child income support is currently means-tested. In Germany, since 1990, basic child income support has been payable for first children irrespective of parental income, but an additional means-tested allowance is payable for second and subsequent children.

All twelve member states of the EU, apart from Greece, operate a system of child income support which is tax free. In Germany, a family's income when it is at the minimum living wage level is not taxable and even the minimum living wage of children since 1990 may no longer be taxed. It has been left to the legislators to implement these principles and to establish the amount which constitutes a child's minimum living income. The Federal Constitutional Court has suggested that the entitlement level for social aid could be used as a guideline for this purpose.

While it is difficult to make inter-country comparisons of child income support across Europe because of the different systems in operation and because of movements in relative exchange rates, Figure 2.1 is presented to give an indication of the different rates of child support in Europe.

Figure 2.1 Child Income Support for First Children in Europe, 1991
Figures shown are monthly amounts of ECUs

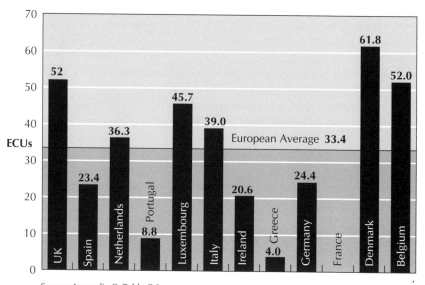

Source: Appendix C, Table C.3
Note: In France there is no child income support for first children but child income support is paid for subsequent children

Figure 2.1 lists, in monthly amounts of ECUs, the child income support paid in EU member states as of July 1991. It is clear that child income support payment levels in Ireland fall below the European average. They are on a par with levels in Spain and above those of Greece and Portugal but significantly below those of the remaining EU member states. In October 1991 the Irish child income support payment for the fourth child was increased to £22.90 or just short of 30 ECUs. In September 1993 Irish child

24

income support payments for the first three children rose to £20 per month and to £23 per month for fourth and subsequent children.

Variations in relation to age expenditure are far from uniform across the EU, but it is clear that globally the costs of child-rearing increase with age and research studies have shown that, from fourteen years onwards, the clothing costs of children are indistinguishable from those of adults (Claude and Moutardier, 1992). Parker (1978) has noted that the costs of child-rearing in the UK are heaviest in the thirteen to eighteen year age group. In Denmark, a special benefit for families with children was introduced in 1987 which is allocated according to the child's age group (zero to three, or four to eighteen). This benefit is universal and tax-free, and is perceived to be a fiscal rather than a social measure. It constitutes one of the elements in a broader political agreement, entitled the "child package" on support for families with children, which came into effect in April 1991 (European Observatory on Family and Policies, 1991).

Chapter 3 - Policy Implications

3. Introduction

From the analysis of the cost of child-rearing in Ireland presented in this report, it is evident that the basic cost of raising a child is not covered adequately by existing child support payments. The study group does not attempt to make any judgement as to what proportion of the cost of child-rearing should be borne by society as a whole, nor what share should be borne by the individual families concerned. It does, however, accept the general principle that some of the costs of raising the next generation should be shared by the entire community. Furthermore, since the child-rearing years form a particular period within most families' life experience, there is a valid argument for the state to become involved in the redistribution of income over the life-cycle of a family; ie taxing income at times where income is sufficient and providing subsistence in times of greater need. Indeed, the same principle is widely accepted and put into practice in regard to the provision of pensions after retirement. If this principle were to be applied in relation to child income support, there are three ways by which this could be achieved within the existing tax and social welfare systems. The advantages and disadvantages of each of the available options is briefly discussed in the following sections.

3.1 Reintroducing child tax allowances

Child tax allowances traditionally formed part of the Irish income tax code, as was the case in most other European countries. However, from the late 1960s onward, they were gradually reduced and finally abolished in 1986. The reason for this change was that tax allowances primarily promote tax equity between couples with children and those without. As they only benefited those in the tax net and, furthermore, benefited those at the higher end of the income distribution more than those at the lower end, they were increasingly seen as an unsuitable means by which to provide child income support to those in greatest need. Clearly, channelling forgone revenue into child benefit or child dependant allowances was of greater benefit to parents at the lower end of the income distribution and hence reflected the underlying shift in importance which was given to this objective. Child tax allowances are not the most suitable means of alleviating poverty as they clearly divert scarce resources away from where they are most needed.

3.2 Increasing child dependant allowances

The main rationale behind the introduction of child dependant allowances was that they provide an efficient way of targeting resources to those in greatest need. As Callan *et al* (1989) show, such payments indeed predominantly benefit those towards the bottom of the income distribution. This was found to be the case not only for means-tested payments, but also for expenditure on contributory benefits. However, increasing child dependant allowances further exacerbates existing unemployment and poverty traps.

These disincentives to work, or unemployment traps, arise where someone who is unemployed would at best be only marginally better off financially in taking up a job. Because welfare payments in Ireland, unlike wages, are differentiated by family size, this problem is most acute for people with children and with low potential net earnings. However, disincentives are unlikely to affect significantly the level of unemployment in Ireland given the current excess of labour supply over demand. Rather, disincentives are more likely to affect the composition of the unemployed. Although about half of those unemployed have no dependants and are thus unlikely to be affected by this particular trap, it constitutes an important issue for larger families disproportionately caught by unemployment; almost half of all families with four or more children have parents who are out of work. Ultimately, this means that a disproportionate number of children grow up in poverty. Indeed Nolan and Farrell have already confirmed that households with children are 1.5 times as likely to be below the poverty line as those without children (1990:89). The incidence of unemployment among those whose parents are unemployed is high; almost half the unemployed aged under 25 have parents out of work. These unemployment traps, by making it difficult for parents who become unemployed to re-enter the workforce, can be a powerful mechanism reinforcing the transmission of unemployment and poverty from one generation to the next.

If Ireland wishes to break the cycle of long-term unemployment and associated welfare dependency, it is essential that the problems of unemployment traps and disincentives to work are tackled. One way of doing this would be to move towards a system of universal child income support which is not dependent on labour market status.

3.3 Increasing child benefit
Child benefit is directed at all families whether the parents are in paid employment or not. In addition, it is paid to mothers, usually the primary caregivers and those with day-to-day responsibility for rearing and budgeting

for children. As a universal payment, it suffers none of the stigmas or other drawbacks associated with means testing. Although child benefit is not directly targeted at poorer families, its targeting could be significantly improved by treating it as taxable income. As Nolan and Farrell (1990) point out, data from the *ESRI 1987 Survey of Households* suggest that only 7.5 per cent of all children receiving child benefit live in households earning over £25,000 a year (1987 figures).

Since increasing child dependant allowances in line with welfare payments would exacerbate unemployment and poverty traps, it is the view of the study group that the best strategy for focusing extra support on the children of low income families would be to increase child benefit and to recoup the amounts going to families who do not need this extra assistance through making child benefit taxable. As the level of child benefit improves, it could gradually be substituted for child dependant allowances. One such detailed proposal has been presented by Callan (1991); he estimated that if child benefit were to be made taxable, an increase in spending of £25m on the scheme could fund a 50 per cent increase in the child benefit rates for those not paying income tax. Families on standard rate tax would be unaffected, while there would be a reduction of between 14-35 per cent in child benefit for higher rate tax payers.

Although families who are evading tax or are otherwise under-assessed for tax would benefit disproportionately from such a change, it is believed that this argues for a tighter tax system, rather than against a restructuring of child support along the lines of the Callan scheme.

3.4 Policy recommendations

State policies in relation to the support of children should reflect the realities of the cost of raising children. In particular, families entirely dependent on the state should receive an income adequate for their children's basic needs. Poorly nourished and poorly dressed children embody an all-too visible mark of poverty. These families need incomes which can also provide for a minimum level of participation in activities that form part of normal development. Society as a whole loses out in the long run if today's children cannot afford to participate in normal recreational and social activities. A clear link has been identified between poverty, deprivation, and problems such as juvenile crime and drug taking (Kennedy Report, 1970; Rottman, 1985; Carmichael, 1981; O'Brien and O'Hare, 1992).

The Basic Minimum Budget Standard described in this report, provides for a diet which is adequate but monotonous, for chainstore clothing, for basic schooling costs, for basic household goods, for personal care, for modest spending on activities, outings, presents and pocket money. Nothing is included in this budget for housing, for home heating, for medical care, for baby-sitting or phone bills. While readers may add or subtract items according to their own view of what is basic, it is clear that state support for families on welfare falls well short of achieving even this basic standard in respect of children of school age and onward. Indeed the shortfall becomes even more marked in the case of teenagers. The study group would argue that a Modest-but-Adequate Budget Standard more accurately reflects the realistic cost of child-rearing although actual amounts may vary from family to family.

As a policy initiative, child income support should more adequately reflect child-rearing costs, particularly for low-income families. With this in mind the authors of this report recommend progressive increases in child benefit payments, with the net benefits focused on lower income families both in and out of employment through assessing child benefits as taxable income. At the same time child dependant payments should be gradually subsumed into this improved child benefit scheme. Given that child poverty and unemployment traps are more acute in larger families, it is suggested that the progressive transition from child dependant allowances should focus initially on payments to larger families. In principle, the long-term aim should be the provision of a universal child support system by the state which is independent of labour force status.

The changing patterns of family formation in Ireland have been documented recently by Fahey (Conference of Major Religious Superiors, 1993). For young unemployed couples, marriage or cohabitation is penalised compared to starting a family while living apart. It is the view of the study group that state child support payments should be neutral in relation to the marital status or choice of living arrangements of the parents, and should not, as at present, provide a financial incentive for parents to live apart. It is thus recommended that child dependant allowances in this respect be progressively harmonised. The introduction of an age-related supplement is also recommended to help reflect the extra costs of raising older children, and it is suggested that twelve years would be the appropriate stage at which to introduce the higher rate.

While food is the largest single item in the budgets, clothing and education costs are significant, particularly for older children. The Back-to-School Clothing and Footwear Allowance only meets a fraction of the costs arising in buying uniforms, autumn footwear, a winter coat, and the cost of schoolbooks. It is recommended that the Back-to-School Clothing and Footwear Allowance be raised to a more realistic level. In addition the reform of the free school-books scheme is recommended in order to ensure that children from lower income homes can meet these costs without hardship and without stigma. The more widespread use of book rental schemes and the development of greater co-ordination between teachers in the setting of textbooks would also ease the problems faced by many parents particularly those within lower income families.

3.5 Summary

- This report advocates redistribution of income over the life-cycle of the family through income taxation in periods of income sufficiency and provision of subsistence in times of greater need.
- State child income support payments should adequately reflect the cost of raising children.
- The long-term objective of a state child support scheme should be a universal system of child income support independent of labour force status.
- Child benefit rates should be increased progressively and be assessed as taxable income.
- Child dependant allowances should be gradually subsumed into this improved child benefit scheme.
- The initial focus of a new child benefit scheme should be on larger families which are disproportionately at risk of poverty.
- Child dependant allowances should be harmonised so that the child benefit scheme can be neutral in relation to the marital status of parents. This is vital in order to negate any financial incentive for parents to live apart.
- Given the higher costs associated with older children this report recommends the introduction of an age-related supplement for children aged twelve and upwards.
- The Back-to-School Clothing and Footwear Allowance should be increased to reflect the needs of school going children.
- To give children from lower income homes the opportunity to acquire the necessary schoolbooks, this report recommends a radical reform of the free schoolbooks scheme.

PART TWO
COSTING INDIVIDUAL EXPENDITURE CATEGORIES

Introduction

Introduction

The cost of a child comprises two distinct components: the indirect or opportunity costs of child-rearing such as loss of income, time costs and the effect of these on social insurance (see Joshi and Owen, 1983; Piachaud, 1984; Joshi, 1987), and the direct costs such as food, clothing and education. Part 2 of this report examines in detail the commodities used by the study group to estimate the direct costs of rearing a child. These direct costs include food, clothing, education, extra-curricular costs, personal care, housing, fuel, household durables, toys and presents, treats and pocket money, and outings and holidays. Other costs which might also be considered direct costs such as housing space, heating and ownership of a car are not included in the costings. It was not possible in the current study to identify what proportion of goods, used in common by the family are directly attributable to children.

Figure 4 Average Weekly Cost of a Child[14]

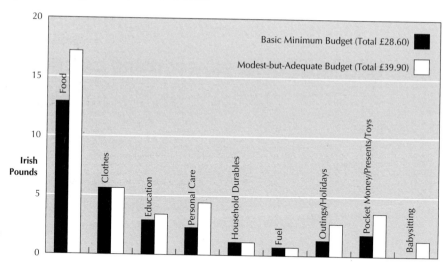

Source: Appendix C, Table C.4
Note: The Modest-but-Adequate figure for education includes pre-school education
Note: All figures are rounded to the nearest 10p

---

[14] Average costs were compiled from the costings for males and females in each age group. Caution should be exercised in interpreting these summary figures as the variance from one age group to another can be significant.

Utilising the budget standard approach discussed in Part 1, Chapters 5 to 14 outline the constituent items in the costed basket of goods and services under each commodity heading. Under each heading costings for a Basic Minimum Budget are presented, and in some cases, costings for a Modest-but-Adequate Budget are also given.

The individual items on the commodity lists were costed in spring 1992 in Irish chainstores. It should be borne in mind, therefore, that all prices are 1992 prices. In selecting items for the Basic Minimum Budget costs were kept to a minimum leaving little room for variety. The Modest-but-Adequate Budget, on the other hand, allowed for more variety and additional expenditure under some commodity headings. For some purposes it may be necessary to add or subtract items from the commodity lists presented here to adjust either to the Basic Minimum Budget or to the Modest-but-Adequate Budget. As items are costed individually, it is possible for the reader to construct alternative estimates to serve better their purpose.

The correlation between age and child-rearing costs, identified in Part 1, clearly highlights the importance of considering consumption costings for each age group separately. Where possible, therefore, commodity costings in the following chapters are subdivided by age group. In addition, where consumption patterns are likely to vary, costings are considered separately for boys and girls.

The following chapter presents a review of existing literature on budget standards and the cost of a child. The literature reviewed were utilised for the development of the budgets and the commodity lists described in later chapters.

PART TWO
COSTING INDIVIDUAL EXPENDITURE CATEGORIES

Chapter 4 - Review of Family Budget Studies

4. Introduction

There are three main approaches to establishing the cost of a child: normative estimates which rely on the judgement of experts to construct budgets; behavioural estimates derived from survey analysis of the patterns of actual spending; and the budget standard approach employed in the current study. In developing the Basic Minimum Budget and the Modest-but-Adequate Budget used here, this study drew extensively on established literature and previous studies in the area of budget standards and other approaches to costing the needs of children. Budgets were constructed based on this documentary research and these were modified with empirical costings and through consultation with a panel of parents. The limitations of the current study prohibited in-depth analysis and extrapolation of the data. Therefore, a brief review of the major budget studies referenced is undertaken in order to place the approach used here in context.

4.1 International family budget studies

A Study of Town Life - Rowntree (1899)

The use of budget standards as an approach to identifying subsistence or poverty levels was pioneered by Rowntree in his study of poverty in York in 1899 (Rowntree, 1901, 1937, 1941). While his aim was not to *define* but to "throw some light upon ... the problem of poverty" (1901:viii) the approach he employed was subsequently adopted by others as a means of defining *minimum acceptable*, and *modest* living standards. Indeed, Rowntree's approach was also used as a basis for Beveridge's proposed National Assistance Scales in 1942.

With the aid of nutritionists and other professionals, Rowntree specified the dietary requirements necessary to maintain "merely physical efficiency" (Rowntree, 1901). He priced the components of these diets and added elements for housing derived from descriptive budget studies as well as minimal expenditure on clothing (Bradshaw *et al*, 1987). In this sense Rowntree's budget is absolute rather than relative as is the case in a number of later studies.

Following Rowntree's work at the turn of the century, the budget standard approach received little attention in the UK until the late 1970s. This, Bradshaw (1993) claims, was partly due to its association with minimum subsistence levels, an unpopular concept in the mid-twentieth century.

Budget standards research, however, did continue to be undertaken in the United States.

City Workers Family Budget - United States Bureau of Labor Statistics (1948)

In the mid 1940s, the United States Bureau of Labor Statistics (US BLS) devised an urban family budget. This initial budget was based on a specific family type, ie an urban family of four persons living in a rented dwelling. The family consisted of an employed husband aged 38, a wife not employed outside the home, and two children, a girl aged eight and a boy aged thirteen. The family budget programme provided annual estimates of the costs of purchasing hypothetical "market baskets" of goods. The US BLS budget differed from Rowntree's work in that a Modest-but-Adequate or "intermediate standard" was introduced in addition to the existing Basic Minimum Budget. This intermediate standard was considered "sufficient to satisfy prevailing standards of what is necessary for health, efficiency, the nurture of children and for participation in community activities" (US Bureau of Labor Statistics, 1948).

The programme was reviewed in the early 1960s, to reflect prevailing standards and to take into account post-war changes in family lifestyles. Market baskets for "lower" and "higher" standards of living for the specified family were added. The goods and services included in both the original and revised budgets, were, insofar as possible, determined on the basis of recognised scientific standards. Where scientific standards did not exist, the quantities and kinds of goods and services included were derived by statistical analysis of post-war consumption data (see Lamale *et al*, 1960). The food quantities and other commodities used in the US BLS budget were those necessary for the specified family and, as such, could not easily be disaggregated for the purposes of the current study to specify amounts required for individual children.

In 1979 The Watts Committee claimed it was impossible to derive an authoritative standard from a technical specification of need based on the judgement of experts. They recommended a change to a behavioural approach based on median expenditure and a move away from the detailed commodity lists of earlier budgets. The report of the Watts Committee defined their median standard as "one that affords full opportunity to participate in contemporary society and the basic options it offers. It is moderate in the sense of lying both above the requirements of survival and decency, and well below levels of luxury as generally understood" (Watts, 1980: viii).

The budgetary work of the US BLS was suspended in 1982 as a result of the budget cuts under the Reagan administration (Bradshaw *et al*, 1987). Some cities in the US and Canada, however, maintained their own budget standards into the 1980s.

New York Community Council Budget Standard (1982)

In 1982 the New York Community Council (NYCC) prepared a Budget Standard loosely based on the Bureau of Labor Statistics budget (1948). The Council used a variety of methods to derive the expenditure amounts required for each component. The food budget was constructed in two stages: first, age- and sex-related dietary needs were specified using an existing dietary schedule; second, items from each major nutrition group were selected according to consumption patterns revealed by New York survey data. Clothing lists were based on survey data which determined quantities and types of clothing. These lists were then priced. Replacement rates for each item were taken into account and average clothes spending was calculated based on the expected lifetime of clothes in the average wardrobe.

Fuel and household equipment were treated on a per capita basis and reflected the additional costs per person of heating, additional furnishings (for example, bedding), and equipment (for example, crockery, cutlery). These were not assumed to vary significantly with age. The personal care and leisure/education budgets were based on survey data, while transport and miscellaneous components were simply allotted a certain percentage of the total. The NYCC Standard excluded medical and housing costs but covered the following categories of expenditure: food, clothing, fuel, personal care, household equipment, leisure/education, transport and miscellaneous. These budget items were costed for an infant aged 0-1 year, for children in the age ranges one to two years, three to five years, six to eight years, nine to eleven years, and for male and female adolescents aged twelve to fourteen years and fifteen to nineteen years.

Cost of a Child - McClements (1978)

McClements's behavioural approach to assessing the cost of a child marked a renewal of interest in family budget costings in the UK. His research employed equivalence scales to study the costs of child-rearing and childless families in the UK in the late 1970s. McClements's findings clearly identified the relationship between the cost of a child and the age of the child (This study is discussed in more detail in Chapter 2 above).

Cost of a Child - Piachaud (1979)

Piachaud, in his study *The Cost of a Child* (1979) used a normative method similar to Rowntree's to outline a modest modern minimum set of requirements for children of different ages. Piachaud's modern minimum aimed to reflect the prevailing social attitudes and standards of the time, and to include some socially defined requirements. However, he acknowledged that this approach was essentially based on his own subjective judgements.

Piachaud's study involved drawing up a list of requirements necessary to maintain a modest minimum lifestyle. He listed items of individual consumption for children of two, five, eight and eleven years of age. These were food, clothing and footwear, school outings, holidays, pocket money, presents and fuel costs specific to each child. Piachaud did not include items of joint consumption such as housing and the child's share of general fuel bills. Piachaud used his estimates to assess the adequacy of child benefit scale rates payable at the time for dependent children in the UK. Ironically Piachaud's "modern minimum" has been condemned as "frugal to the point of inhumanity" (Lynes, 1979), despite being above the relevant welfare rates for children.

In his 1979 study, Piachaud only covered four age bands of children (two, five, eight and eleven years of age). He omitted babies because, he argued, their requirements varied greatly depending on whether it was a first or subsequent child. He also left out teenagers because he considered that there was less agreement regarding their needs than regarding those of younger children. In a later study, Piachaud (1981) adopted a behavioural approach to estimating the costs of teenagers, aged 13 to 15 since given the variability of views about what teenagers need, he considered that it would be pointless to attempt to list a set of their requirements. Thus he asserted that a behavioural approach was more suitable for measuring the costs of teenagers.

In using an adapted modern version of Rowntree's approach, Piachaud has been influenced by recent research on poverty and deprivation (see Townsend, 1979; Mack and Lansley, 1985). The emphasis has shifted from physical requirements for mere survival to the principle of a minimum amount of resources required to lead a normal life.

Babies and Money - Roll (1986)

In *Babies and Money*, Roll (1986) employed the normative approach to estimating the cost of a baby. She reviewed a variety of expert estimates on these costs. These were drawn up by parents' magazines, newspapers and insurance companies. She identified four areas of direct cost: maternity, outlay on the baby, optional extras (toys, safety equipment, tumble drier, etc.), and "running costs". Estimates for clothing and equipment for babies in magazine articles were £700-£800. The cost of baby foods and other week to week spending had been estimated at £575 for a year by *Parents* magazine.

Budgeting on Benefit - Bradshaw and Morgan (1987)

Bradshaw and Morgan's *Budgeting on Benefit: the Consumption of Families on Social Security* (1987) illustrated the living standard which could be afforded on the supplementary benefit scale rates in the UK, by drawing up a detailed list of goods and services that two types of families on supplementary benefit could buy with their money. Bradshaw and Morgan used available data from the *Family Finances Survey*, a once-off survey of low-income families in the UK, as a guide in their allocation of income for food, clothing, fuel, alcohol, tobacco, household goods, transport, services and other goods. All dietary budgets were subjected to a nutritional assessment.

Cost of Child-rearing - Mitchell and Cooke (1988)

Mitchell and Cooke's article, "The Cost of Child-rearing" (1988) reviewed in detail various studies and methods of deriving the cost of children. Using the 1982 Family Expenditure Survey and the Retail Price Index they presented a modified version of the New York Consumer Council's budget standard to fit the British context in the late 1980s.

Poor Families - Stitt (1989)

Stitt (1989) conducted a study similar to Bradshaw and Morgan's study (1987) in Northern Ireland (*Poverty, Income and Supplementary Benefit*, 1989). He also described living standards for poor families. Stitt related the weekly scale rates for supplementary benefit to the cost of meeting basic family needs in Northern Ireland.

Modest-but-Adequate Family Budget - Family Budget Unit, York (1990)

The Family Budget Unit (FBU) in York was formed in 1985 and aimed to research the economic requirements and consumer preferences of families of different composition, for the main expenditure components of a typical family budget. The FBU agreed to concentrate on a "modest-but-adequate" standard, and to avoid attempting to estimate a poverty line. They decided to "leave it to others to decide what items the recipients of social security benefits should or should not be expected to forego" (*Family Budget Unit Working Paper No. 1*, 1990: 3).

The work of the FBU concentrated on family as opposed to child budgets. However, "baskets of goods and services" were devised for a girl aged four and a boy aged ten. The FBU concentrated on family budgets to avoid the difficulty of trying to extract child costs from the joint consumption of the whole family for certain goods such as fuel and household goods and services. The FBU study established model budgets for six family units;

- a single man (aged 30 years)
- a single woman (aged 72 years)
- two adults (man 34, woman 32)
- two adults, two children (man 34, woman 32, girl four, boy ten)
- two adults, two children (man 37, woman 35, boy ten, girl sixteen)
- one adult, two children (woman 32, girl four, boy ten)

The work of the FBU combines information on observed expenditure patterns with expert prescriptions. Technical groups of home economists, nutritionists, and social scientists interested in domestic economy were asked to determine: what items to include; quantity of items; price; how the expenditure is to be established; and lifetimes of items (so that replacement costs could be calculated). The work of the FBU also draws on the UK *Family Expenditure Survey*. For all items, except clothing where specific lists for individual children are given, expenditure relates to households or families and not to individuals.

Cost of a Child - Oldfield and Yu (1993)
Oldfield and Yu's study under the FBU in York also employed the budget standard approach in assessing the cost of a child. Similar to the current study, two budget standards were employed: a low-cost budget and a modest-but-adequate budget. The component items in the budgets were chosen by a group of experts and were informed by what people actually spend their money on. In addition the low-cost budget was informed by the *Breadline Britain* survey which determined what people thought were necessities. The components included: housing, fuel, food, clothing, household goods and services, childcare, transport, leisure goods and services, personal care and pocket money. The equivalence scales identified by Oldfield and Yu were compared with those of McClements (1978) and Piachaud (1979).

4.2 Irish family budget studies
Minimum Income for Adults - Commission on Social Welfare (1986)
The Commission on Social Welfare used different approaches to establish an appropriate minimum income for adults, but did not do any similar work to establish the cost of children. The Commission's report presents different equivalence scales for children derived from expenditure studies conducted in the UK, USA, EU and Australia. These equivalence scales give the costs of children as varying from 16.9 per cent to 35 per cent of a reference couple (100 per cent). All these studies revealed higher costs for older children.

Cost of Children - Conniffe and Keogh (1988)
Conniffe and Keogh's (1988) survey of equivalence scales and the cost of children examined the concept of "equivalent income" in families with and without children. Equivalent income is the income at which households with a child enjoy the same living standard as a reference household without children (this study is discussed in more detail in Chapter 2 above).

Low Income Food Budget - Lee and Gibney (1989)
Lee and Gibney (*Patterns of Food and Nutrient Intake in a Suburb of Dublin with Chronically High Unemployment*, 1989) carried out a study of food consumption among low-income families in Tallaght. One purpose of the study was to provide data on the divergence between the current eating habits of the respondents, and the dietary guidelines of the Department of Health. For children under eighteen of both sexes, mean nutrient intakes were found to be either equal to, or greater than, the recommended dietary allowances (RDAs) for protein and carbohydrates; there were some deficiencies in vitamin C and iron. Lee and Gibney calculated that the weekly cost of meeting a twelve-year-old child's dietary needs, even at the low level they describe, actually exceeds the full financial allotment under social welfare provisions for children of parents in receipt of unemployment assistance.

Cost of Education - National Parents Council (1990 and 1991)
The National Parents Council (Primary) study *The Cost of Free Education* detailed a survey conducted on the cost to parents of free primary education in Ireland. Questionnaires were sent to the parents' associations of 1,000 schools. The report outlined some of the categories of cost which parents must meet in order for their child to participate in the normal curricular and extra-curricular activities associated with being in school. These costs

included fundraising activities by parents for the child's school; costs of books and uniforms; costs of school facilities, photocopying, art materials, exams; extra-curricular activities and school tours.

The National Parents Council (Post-primary) published a case study on the cost to parents of educating a child from infant class up to the end of sixth year in secondary school (*Textbooks: What a price*, 1991). The study focused on selected schools in Tipperary Town. The study looked at the year-by-year costs of uniforms, books, equipment, school bags, extra-curricular activities, bus fares, lunch allowances, sports gear, etc.

Cost of Education - PAUL Project (1991)
Based on a survey of 99 low-income families in Limerick, the publication *Educational Costs and Welfare Provisions for Low-Income Families* (1991) gave details of direct and indirect costs of school for these families, and compared the results with welfare provisions.

Welfare Family Budgets and Average Income Budgets - Murphy-Lawless (1992)
Murphy-Lawless's study, *The Adequacy of Income and Family Expenditure* (1992) followed the approach developed by Bradshaw and Morgan. She used existing aggregate data from the *Household Budget Survey* to examine the actual living standards achieved by families. Special subsamples were drawn from the *1987 Household Budget Survey*, of welfare families with two children ("welfare" family), and families with two children and earnings between £200-£250 a week ("average" family). The study constructed detailed shopping baskets of items that could be afforded by a welfare family and by an average family. These shopping baskets of the two subsamples were based on average actual spending under broad headings including food, clothes, drink and tobacco, fuel and light, housing repairs and household durables, transport and services. The study noted those areas where welfare families were likely to cut back on commodities compared to average families in order to live within their incomes.

COSTING INDIVIDUAL EXPENDITURE CATEGORIES

Chapter 5 - Food

5. Introduction

This chapter details the food costs used in this report under a Basic Minimum standard and a Modest-but-Adequate standard (see Chapter 2, Table 2.1). The derivation and composition of the food budgets are explained, along with any additions or adjustments made to arrive at the final food costs. Finally, the overall costs are compared with the findings of other reports.

5.1 Budgetary standards

Basic Minimum Budget Standard

Food, as the largest single item in most household budgets, accounts for almost half of the spending under the Basic Minimum Budget and a similar proportion under the Modest-but-Adequate Budget (see Figure 4 above). The Basic Minimum Budget Standard for food, as presented in Table 5.1 below, is a conservative one, based on nutritious but monotonous diets consumed by children in the low-income families in Lee & Gibney's study (1989). Minor additions have been made to ensure that intakes of iron and vitamin C are in line with recommended levels. Adjustments were also made to take account of variations in recommended calorie intakes across the age ranges in question.

Figure 5.1 Weekly Cost of Food

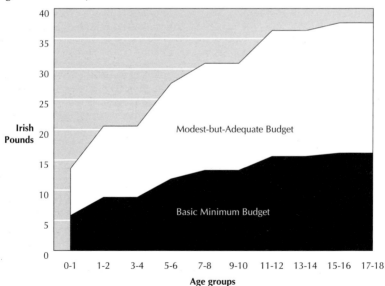

Source: Table 5.1 & Table 5.2

48

Table 5.1 Weekly Cost of Food - Basic Minimum Standard, 1992

Age/ Gender	0-1 £	1-2 £	3-4 £	5-6 £	7-8 £	9-10 £	11-12 £	13-14 £	15-16 £	17-18 £
Boys	5.80	9.05	9.05	12.78	14.36	14.36	17.50	17.50	18.60	18.60
Girls	5.80	8.58	8.58	10.90	12.16	12.16	13.66	13.66	13.66	13.66
Average	5.80	8.81	8.81	11.84	13.26	13.26	15.58	15.58	16.13	16.13

Modest-But-Adequate Budget Standard

The diets in the Murphy-Lawless study (1992, Tables 5 and 6) contain detailed itemised menu lists chosen after discussions with the Ballymun Development Co-operative, and also fitted within food spending totals from the *Household Budget Survey*. When the diets for welfare dependent families were compared with the diets of average income families, Murphy-Lawless found that families on average income spend about one-third more on food than families on social welfare; welfare families in her study spent £44.95 (25%) of their weekly income on food, in comparison to the average income families who spent £60.08 (34%). The Modest-but-Adequate Budget used here is derived from the Basic Minimum Budget on the basis of a one-third differential. This extra expenditure would provide for a more varied diet than the nutritious but monotonous diet outlined in the Basic Minimum Budget. The more varied diet purchased under the Modest-but-Adequate standard could cost up to £11 a week for a pre-school child and up to £21.50 a week for a teenager. Table 5.2 below represents the weekly costs of food under the Modest-but-Adequate Budget standard.

Table 5.2 Weekly Cost of Food - Modest-but-Adequate Standard, 1992

Age/ Gender	0-1 £	1-2 £	3-4 £	5-6 £	7-8 £	9-10 £	11-12 £	13-14 £	15-16 £	17-18 £
Boys	7.73	12.07	12.07	17.04	19.15	19.15	23.33	23.33	24.80	24.80
Girls	7.73	11.44	11.44	14.53	16.21	16.21	18.21	18.21	18.21	18.21
Average	7.73	11.75	11.75	15.79	17.68	17.68	20.77	20.77	21.51	21.51

5.2 Nutrition

Nutrition needs

Food can be divided into four main groups: (i) the meat group, including meat, fish, eggs, cheese, beans and other protein rich foods; (ii) fruit and vegetables; (iii) bread and cereals, including rice, pasta and potatoes; and (iv) the milk group, including cheese and yogurt. For a child, the Department of Health recommends a daily diet which includes two servings from the meat group, four servings from the fruit and vegetables group, four servings from the bread and cereals group, and three from the milk group. Additional helpings from the bread and cereal group and the milk group are recommended for teenagers. In general, a balanced and varied diet with sufficient protein and calories will contain enough of the other recommended nutrients, vitamins and minerals.

Table 5.3 Recommended Dietary Allowances by Age

	RDA kCal Boys	RDA kCal Girls
Age 1-3	1300	1300
Age 4-6	1700	1700
Age 7-10	2000	2000
Age 11-14	2800	2100
Age 15-18	2900	2100

Source: McGee and Fitzgerald, 1988.

In examining budget standards for food, it is important to look at the kind of food people actually buy and eat, rather than devising a nutritious diet of items that rarely feature on Irish tables. In costing a basic diet, the study group was influenced by the average diet purchased by a sample of low-income Dublin families, in a recent study by two nutritionists, Lee and Gibney (1989). The basic food budget selected in this report is largely based on the food consumed by children of different ages in the Lee and Gibney study. Their diets satisfy three criteria:

- nutritionally adequate (subject to minor adjustments)
- based on real consumption patterns
- minimum cost.

Food needs vary by age, and boys generally require more food than girls. Recommended dietary allowances (RDAs) for a variety of nutrients have been published by the Health Promotion Unit of the Department of Health, and are designed to cover the needs of 97.5 per cent of the population in any given age/sex group (*Nutrition Health Promotion Framework for Action*, Health Promotion Unit, 1991, Appendix v). The officially recommended diets based on these allowances are stated in broad terms and are not readily turned into food baskets which could be costed.

Nutritional standard
The Lee and Gibney children's diets have been assessed as nutritionally adequate based on recommended minimum and maximum intakes of nutrients, subject to minor modifications. They satisfied requirements for protein and calorie consumption, but iron and vitamin C intakes were below recommended levels. To compensate for these deficiencies the study group has made minor changes to bring the diets into balance. Brown bread was substituted for half the white bread allocation, a portion of liver was substituted once a week for an equivalent portion of beefburger, and half an orange a day was added for those aged under four years, and a full orange a day for those aged four and over. It appears that these adjustments would improve vitamin C, iron and fibre intake, without affecting the protein or calorie composition of the diets (Lee & Gibney, 1989) (see Appendix A for costings of dietary modifications).

The Lee and Gibney diets provide an adequate amount of protein and calories for each age group which at least reach the Department of Health's recommended levels. If a diet with lower calorie levels was specified, it is likely that, in practice, the balance would be altered and deficiencies in other nutrients could emerge. A lower calorie intake might mean a diet with less milk consumption and a lower intake of calcium.

5.3 Average food consumption
Detailed diets, showing daily consumption in grams of the main food items, are listed in Table 5.4 below. The lists include the average consumption of

these items in the sample studied by Lee and Gibney, together with the adjustments made to improve nutritional balance. The cost has been updated to February 1992 prices. The food lists are given for children in four broad age groups: age one to under four; age four to under seven; age seven to under eleven; and age eleven to under eighteen. Different figures are shown for boys and girls, with boys generally consuming more than girls, and the difference in food intake becoming more pronounced for older children.

5.4 Dietary costings

The Lee and Gibney diets were bought predominantly by families on very low incomes with no money to spare (1989:8-9, Tables 2.3 and 2.7)[15]. They are monotonous with little variety, and can hardly be seen as extravagant. They would seem to represent the minimum cost of providing food for a family in Ireland. To quote from their study:

"The range of foods consumed was very limited and there was little variation in the food eaten from week to week ... Diets were characterised by high consumption of milk, bread and potatoes, and a low consumption of fresh fruit and vegetables. Economics clearly played a role in the types of meat consumed which were of the cheapest variety, eg poor quality beef, mince, sausages, frozen beefburgers, chicken and bacon ... Tinned peas and beans were the most commonly used vegetables, but carrots were also regularly eaten in stews. Fresh fruit was considered a luxury; a bag of ten apples or oranges was the usual weekly purchase of fruit, whatever the family size" (Lee and Gibney, 1989:74).

The costings were taken from the Lee and Gibney study and updated by the food component in the Consumer Price Index. Additional items (liver,

---

[15]Three-quarters of the families in the Lee and Gibney study (1989) were on welfare payments; many had recurring debts for basic living expenses.

[16]These lists are based on Lee and Gibney (1989), Tables 5.2, 5.4, 5.6 and 5.8. The figures are updated to February 1992 prices, using movements in the food component of the CPI since their fieldwork was carried out. The adjustments made to the diet were priced at Crazy Prices, Sandyford, Dublin. Brown sliced bread at 81p per 800g loaf was substituted for half the white bread, costing 49p per 800g for own-brand bread. A portion of liver once a week, at £2.39 a kg, was substituted for own-brand beefburgers at 69p for four. Half an orange a day for under fours and an orange a day for older children was added to the diet, with oranges priced at eight for 98p. The additional costs were computed using the figures for average daily consumption of bread and meat in different age groups shown in Lee & Gibney.

Table 5.4 Average Food consumption of Children[16] (in grams)

Age/ Food	1-3 boy grams	1-3 girl grams	4-6 boy grams	4-6 girl grams	7-11 boy grams	7-11 girl grams	11-18 boy grams	11- 18 girl grams
Bread	79	70	144	150	220	145	307	178
Milk	604	626	661	492	622	592	592	527
Cheese	3	7	7	13	9	3	13	11
Butter	13	14	21	18	25	16	37	20
Margarine	4	2	0	5	5	3	7	5
Breakfast cereal	27	24	33	28	36	30	36	22
Fresh meat	21	21	40	25	35	40	53	50
Processed meat	22	19	41	25	40	28	59	43
Fish	6	9	6	8	8	8	10	5
Eggs	18	17	25	20	22	20	26	25
Chips	13	12	35	16	36	29	58	41
Other potatoes	92	83	94	113	121	125	187	97
Peas/beans	37	40	54	53	43	45	63	36
Other vegetables	11	12	15	14	20	21	24	44
Orange	7	14	22	9	16	19	16	14
Other fruit	60	41	95	34	51	115	43	41
Fruit Juice	4	0	17	10	8	27	7	2
Sugar	17	17	24	18	36	25	42	46
Cakes/Biscuits	41	23	26	38	39	33	47	27
Sweets/chocolates	26	15	39	32	44	36	66	61
Soft drinks	61	62	163	50	86	95	104	90
Avg.daily Kcal	**1,619**	**1,524**	**2,214**	**1,857**	**2,500**	**2,095**	**2,190**	**2,381**
Cost	£	£	£	£	£	£	£	£
Updated Cost 1992	8.49	8.02	11.68	9.82	13.16	11.00	16.74	12.50
Add adjustments	0.56	0.56	1.10	1.08	1.20	1.10	1.34	1.16
Total	**9.05**	**8.58**	**12.78**	**10.90**	**14.36**	**12.16**	**18.08**	**13.66**

Note: Sampling errors for some of these items represent the variation in consumption reflected by sub-samples in each age group.

oranges and brown bread) were costed at a nationwide retail outlet and added to the Lee and Gibney figures.

Table 5.5 Weekly Cost of Basic Diet, 1992*

Age	Adjusted cost for Boys £	Adjusted cost for Girls £
1 - under 4	9.05	8.58
4 - under 7	12.78	10.90
7 - under 11	14.36	12.16
11 - under 18	18.08	13.66

* Adjusted to provide minimum nutritional requirements.

The figures shown in Table 5.5, if anything, are more likely to underestimate than overestimate the cost of food for children of different ages and a diet with greater variety would undoubtedly be more expensive. In addition, an estimate has been made by the study group of the cost of food for babies under one year, based mainly on the cost of recommended quantities of baby milk. This works out at £5-£6 a week and is described in the following section.

Baby food

The diet of young babies is very different from that of older children but by the age of one year a baby will take fewer special foods and move on to consuming ordinary milk. The cost of baby foods will vary depending on whether a baby is breast-fed or bottle fed, whether the baby has moved on to solids, and by age and size of the baby. There is also waste with baby foods as they cannot be safely reheated.

Manufacturers of a proprietary baby milk consulted by the study group estimated the weekly cost of formula milk, based on the recommended intake at each age, as follows: for a child aged three months, £5.22 a week; aged six months £4.90 a week; aged nine months, £3.68; and aged twelve months, £2.45. These are obviously approximate figures as the cost will vary from brand to brand and from outlet to outlet.

Babies on solids drink less milk, and would eat a combination of portions of the family's food, and of bought baby foods. Items like yogurt, banana, infant biscuits, or fruit juice, which may be part of an older baby's diet, have not been specifically priced into the present study. It is suggested that a modest estimate of the cost of table food for a baby, plus occasionally purchased ready-made baby dinners, would amount to about 30p a day. That amount, for example, would buy one jar of baby food or one-and-a-half standard cartons of yogurt.

These estimates calculate the cost of feeding a baby as varying from about £5.20 a week for a baby of three months on milk only, to about £5.80 for a baby of nine months on a combination of milk and solid foods. In round terms, they amount to £5-£6 per week, and are comparable with the £7 per week for a baby's food budget estimated in the Mitchell and Cooke study (1988) when converted to current Irish prices.

Food costs for older children
The age ranges in the Lee and Gibney study (1989) are broad, particularly for teenagers; in reality, the transition from lower to higher food intake would be smoother than the previous estimates suggest. A better picture of food costs for teenagers may be estimated by adjusting for the different calorie requirements of older and younger teenagers. The recommended dietary allowances for boys suggest that older teenage boys need about 3 per cent more food than the average required for the eleven to eighteen age group as a whole, and younger teenage boys about 3 per cent less. Making this adjustment gives the estimated weekly cost of this food budget as £17.50 for a boy aged eleven to fourteen, and £18.60 for a boy aged fifteen to eighteen.

When the costs in Table 5.5 are adjusted to take account of the information outlined above, the calculations result in the costs represented in Table 5.1. The underlying averages in the Lee and Gibney study (1989) on which the above estimates are based are, of course, subject to sampling error, and the estimates must be seen as approximate rather than showing precise costs. The figures suggest a small difference in the food costs of boys and girls up to age eleven, and a significant widening of the gap thereafter. The recommended dietary allowances for boys and girls are the same up to age eleven, although more active children (who are more often boys) may need more calories. The gap between the sexes in food costs in the teenage years reflects exactly the differences in recommended daily calories.

5.5 Comparison of results

The cost of the present study's Basic Minimum Budget Standard for food is shown alongside those of Piachaud (1979) and Mitchell and Cooke (1988) in Table 5.6[17]. One of these, the Piachaud food budget (1979), was based on the quantities contained in a "low-cost" diet reported earlier in a US nutrition study. This diet, which may be described as frugal, contains larger amounts of milk and vegetables (low-cost foods), and less meat and sweets (high-cost or nutritionally unnecessary food), than many children actually consume. In the second study (Mitchell and Cooke, 1988), the New York Consumer Council Family Budgets for 1982 were presented in UK prices and have been adjusted to current Irish price levels. This diet includes items from each nutrition group according to consumption patterns revealed by New York survey data.

The food budget in the current study, although constructed without reference to these studies, gives the same order of cost in corresponding age groupings.

Table 5.6 Basic Budget Standard for Food, Irish Prices 1992.

Piachaud		Mitchell & Cooke		The current study	
Ages	£	Ages	£	Ages	£
2	8.40	1-2	8.35	1-2	8.81
5	9.50	3-5	10.00	3-6	10.32
8	12.50	6-8	13.10	7-8	13.26
11	12.90	9-11	16.30	9-12	14.42
n.a	n.a	12-14	15.40 - 17.40	13-14	15.58
n.a	n.a	15-19	15.40 - 19.00	15-18	16.13

Sources: *1987 Household Budget Survey*, Table 8, (1989); Piachaud, 1979; Mitchell & Cooke, 1988.

Household Budget Survey

Average figures for food spending from the *1987 Household Budget Survey* show spending by families rather than individuals. Table 5.7 and Figure 5.2

---

[17] Costs from Piachaud and Mitchell and Cooke's studies are adjusted to 1992 Irish prices. The adjustments were made using the change in the UK Consumer Price Index for food items, and an exchange rate of 93p per £1 sterling prevailing at end 1991.

below give average weekly spending by stage in the family cycle and by family size, adjusted to 1992 prices by use of the food component of the CPI (Consumer Price Index).

Figure 5.2 Average Weekly Food Spending by Family Cycle, 1992

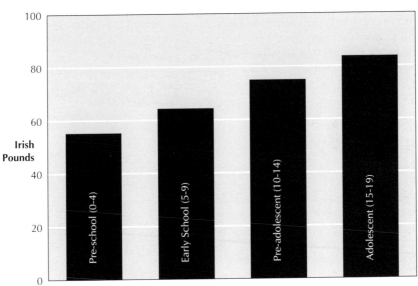

Source: Appendix C, Table C.5

The *Household Budget Survey* figures on average weekly spending by family cycle show a clear increase in spending on food throughout the family life-cycle stages (Figure 5.2). This would appear to support this study's findings in relation to the age-related increases in spending on food for children (Table 5.1).

As one would expect, the average weekly spending on food increases with family size. The derived marginal expenditure per additional child, calculated from *Household Budget Survey* (1989) figures, illustrates the additional spending per child when children are present in a family (Table 5.7). The derived marginal expenditure per additional child indicates that economies of scale may perhaps exist between first and second children, or indeed between first children and second or third children. However, the derived marginal expenditure for fourth or subsequent children is considerably higher than for lower birth order children. It is assumed for the purpose of this study therefore, that no real economies of scale exist in food spending for larger families. A similar assumption was made by Conniffe and Keogh (1988) in their research into equivalence scales. The issue of food economies occurring in larger families was discussed with the panels of mothers consulted by the study group. In their experience, little if any economies were found to be occurring in this particular area of expenditure.

Table 5.7 Average Weekly Food Spending by Family Size, 1992

Family Type	1992 Prices £	(Derived Marginal Expenditure per Additional Child)
Couple	47.54	-
Couple, 1 child	55.15	(7.61)
Couple, 2 children	61.56	(6.41)
Couple, 3 children	68.23	(6.67)
Couple, 4 children	78.34	(10.11)

Source: *1987 Household Budget Survey* (1989), Table 9. Consumer Price Index.

There is a noticeable difference in the *Household Budget Survey* figures on food expenditure per child (Table 5.7) and those estimated in the current study (Table 5.1). This discrepancy is due to the use of different methodologies; this study uses a budget standard approach (costing the actual expenditure on children), whereas the *Household Budget Survey* data is derived using a differential cost approach. Moreover, this differential cost approach estimates the cost of a child as the *extra* amount a family spends for each additional child, but does not show what proportion of the spending is on the child. The difference between what a couple with a child spend and what a couple without a child spend, cannot adequately represent the cost of a child. Any claim to the contrary would assume that the amount a couple spend on themselves remains constant, and that irrespective of income or the presence of a child they would not cut back on their own consumption. Indeed, Lee and Gibney (1989), in their study of food intake in an area of unemployment, reported that:

"Most of the family income was spent on food and necessities for the children who were unquestionably the main focus of attention. Parents seemed to be prepared to make any sacrifice necessary to see that the children were not 'short' of anything. Often, however, this meant severe hardship particularly for the mother who usually went without herself" (Lee and Gibney, 1989:73).

5.6 Summary

- The weekly cost of food under the Basic Minimum Budget standard ranges from £5.80 for a baby to £16.13 for a teenager aged over fifteen years. Under the Modest-but-Adequate Budget standard these costs range from £7.73 to £21.51.
- Food consumption, and correspondingly food costs, increase with age. This relationship is particularly strong for boys.
- With the exception of children aged under one year, the cost of food in all age groups is greater for boys than for girls. This differential further increases with age.
- There appear to be few economies of scale in food budgets for large families.
- In low-income families it would appear that the food budget is composed of the child's food budget and a reduced food budget for parents.

Chapter 6 - Clothing

6. Introduction

This chapter considers the clothing and footwear commodity group. Items and costings are presented for a Basic Minimum Budget for clothing and are compared with basic clothing budgets prepared for other studies.

6.1 Budgetary standards

Basic Minimum Budget Standard

The cost of a basic clothes list for each age group is shown in Figure 6.1 below. These lists include school uniforms, but not sports kits (these items are costed under the education and extra-curricular commodity group, see Chapter 7). Moreover, a communion outfit at age seven to eight, and a confirmation outfit at age eleven to twelve, have not been included[18]. While spending on individual girls would be slightly higher, reflecting their more varied wardrobes, their clothes are more likely to have some useful life left when they are outgrown than is clothing worn by boys.

In constructing a clothes budget, wardrobe lists were made for different age groups of boys and girls and assumptions were made about when clothes would be outgrown or outworn. Guidance was gained from other budget studies which gave wardrobe lists and expected useful lifespans for clothing. These studies included the York Family Budget Unit (1990), Bradshaw and Morgan (1987) and Murphy-Lawless (1992). Average weekly spending on clothing was estimated by dividing the cost of items in the chosen wardrobe by the expected weekly lifespan of the items. The wardrobes constructed for the different age groups reflect the study group's best judgement as to basic clothes needs for children in different age groups. Therefore, the variation in the clothes chosen, or in their quality, obviously affects their useful life. Common sense indicates that poor-quality cheap items may last only half the time of better quality items, and that a child with two jumpers will wear them out roughly twice as fast as the child with four. The lifetimes for the different clothing items are adapted from those used by the York Family Budget Unit study to reflect the somewhat smaller wardrobe chosen. The clothes have been priced in national chainstores (Dunnes Stores, Penneys[19]) and are taken from the middle price, medium quality range (detailed clothing lists and estimated lifetimes are given in Appendix B).

---

[18] A communion outfit at £104 would cost £2 per week at age seven. This would add £1 per week to the cost of the clothing budget for the seven- to eight-year-old age group. A confirmation outfit at £144 would cost £2.75 per week at age twelve, resulting in an addition of £1.38 per week to the eleven- to twelve-year-old age group.

Figure 6.1 Weekly Cost of Clothes - Basic Minimum Standard, 1992

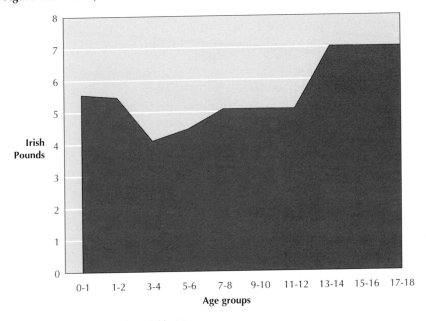

Source: Appendix C, Table C.6

Families on low incomes are likely to wear their clothes for longer, and to rely more on second-hand clothing or hand-me-downs. The survey conducted by the St Vincent de Paul Society as part of its submission to the Commission on Social Welfare (Williams & Whelan, 1985) showed that low-income families are more likely to spend a £50 gift on new clothes for their children than in any other way; while 24 per cent of respondents said they would spend a £50 gift on buying clothes for children, this rose to 37 per cent in families with four or more children (Williams & Whelan, 1985, Table 6.2: 63). Recent work by the Economic and Social Research Institute looking at the "enforced lack" of certain items among poor families shows a third of families living below the 50 per cent poverty line reporting an enforced lack of new clothes (Callan,

---

[19] Most clothes for the under twelves were priced in Dunnes Stores in The Square in Tallaght, Co Dublin, with additional information from Dunnes Stores head office. Other clothes for this age group were priced in Penneys of Dundrum, Dublin. Teenage clothes were priced in Penneys, Rathfarnham, Dublin. Footwear was priced in Boylan's shoe store, Dundrum, and sports gear in Lifestyle, Dundrum. Where there was a choice, items were selected from the medium price, medium quality range.

1991). Wearing second-hand or worn-out clothes is a visible sign of poverty. The study group considers that a budget standard for children should allow for each child of school-going age to have new clothes of his or her own.

6.2 Clothing requirements and lifespan

The lifespan of any garment will vary with the rate of growth of an individual child, and with how hard she or he is on wearing out clothes. Individual parents, and indeed children, may vary in their assessments as to when a garment is no longer wearable because it is worn out. The lifetimes presented in this study must be taken as indicative, not precise; a variation of 20 per cent plus or minus would affect the resulting budget figures by a corresponding amount. To quote the York Family Budget Unit study:

"The lifespan of clothes is particularly difficult to estimate, because it is dependent on a large number of interrelated factors, and the decision about how long an item should be kept is very subjective. However, it is possible to identify factors affecting lifespan as including the following:
1. The quantity of the particular item in question
2. How frequently the item of clothing is worn
3. The type and quality of the fabric and its durability to wear and laundering
4. The quality of the manufacturing processes
5. How frequently the garment is washed
6. The growth rate of a child."
(Family Budget Unit, 1990).

For very young children, clothes are likely to be outgrown before they are outworn, resulting in higher unit costs as a result of the shorter periods over which the cost can be spread. The sizes in which baby clothes are sold, for example up to three months, three to six months, six months to one year, give a guide to how long an item will fit the average baby. Many of the baby and toddler clothes could be passed on to younger brothers or sisters. As children grow older clothes are worn for longer, consequently the cost of clothing an individual child diminishes in the pre-school years (see Figure 6.1). However, the likelihood of any useful wear being left in these clothes also diminishes sharply. Quite apart from this, however, the sex, shape, and spacing of children will strongly influence whether clothes can be handed down.

None of the studies examined presented different lifespans for clothing for boys and girls. Boys generally wear out their clothes more quickly than girls, so that lifespans for items like trousers will be shorter than lifespans of equivalent items for girls. One mother of a ten year old boy reported that a pair of trousers lasts him six to eight weeks with torn knees, and that she buys three tracksuit bottoms to every top. An additional allowance for wear and tear on trousers has been made for boys in the current study. Nonetheless, the clothes budget for girls remains consistently higher than for boys due for the most part to the fact that girls clothing is more expensive. The gender differential is greatest in the teenage years (£1.11 per week), but the differential is also relatively large during the first six months (£1.01). This decreases in the pre-school years and remains relatively unchanged throughout the primary school years (£0.09).

In deciding quantities and lifespans for clothing in this study, the research was mainly guided by UK studies with some adaptation in standards. It must be recognised, however, that in Ireland, a generally wetter climate than the UK, children may need to have more jumpers or trousers simply to be sure of clothes being adequately dried. There obviously will be an inverse relationship between the number of jumpers, how often they are worn, and how soon they wear out.

School uniforms
The list of trousers, skirts, blouses or shirts, and jumpers in the wardrobes is assumed to include school uniforms bought from chain stores, which are acceptable in many schools. Where schools specify a particular design of uniform or a particular outlet, costs could be significantly higher[20].

Clothes for special occasions
It is a widespread custom in Ireland to dress children in new clothes for Christmas, and to dress all the children in new clothes for a family occasion such as a first communion or a confirmation. The new clothes bought for special occasions have not been included as a separate heading in the clothes budget. The study group considers that clothes bought at these times will form part of the usual wardrobe described below. First communion and confirmation outfits would not, however, form part of the normal wardrobe, and thus are costed as an addition to the budget. Based on figures presented

---

[20] The National Parents' Council (1990) have costed a uniform for a five-year-old of two shirts, a skirt, and a jumper at £31 in a specialist store, compared to the cost of £20.80 in the present study for a similar outfit in a chainstore.

in the PAUL Project study undertaken in Limerick (1991), the cost of a first communion outfit is estimated at £104 and of a confirmation outfit at £144. These costs can be added to the clothes budgets at age seven to eight, and age twelve if required. The purchase of clothes for school or for special occasions causes a significant clustering of expenditure at these times and can be particularly difficult for families on low incomes.

6.3 Clothing costs

A series of detailed clothing budgets have been devised for different age groups. Clothing lists for children were compiled based on those of the York Family Budget Unit budgets (1990), but these budgets were modified to suit Irish circumstances. In some cases the Bradshaw and Morgan (1987) and Murphy-Lawless (1992) studies were also taken into consideration. As none of the studies contained a list of clothing for babies this was compiled by the study group in consultation with a group of mothers.

Clothing for babies

For babies, estimated lifespans for clothing have been used based on how soon the baby would grow out of the different clothing articles. Most clothes will have some degree of useful life left in them after they have been outgrown, and thus the additional clothing needs of a second baby may be negligible. A first baby aged up to six months would cost about £6.37 a week to clothe by the current study standard, while from six to twelve months, this figure drops to about £4.72. While it would be expected that clothing costs would rise again for the toddler, with the necessity to wear shoes and the need also for increased amounts of clothing for wear outdoors, this increase is likely to be counterbalanced by the longer period over which the cost of the clothes can be spread (see section 6.2 above).

Clothing for children of school age

Most of the studies examined relied on a sample family of one boy and one girl. In drawing up a clothing list for each age group for the purposes of the current study, decisions were guided both by these studies and by the discussions held with panels of mothers. The expected lifespans of clothing related to the general size of the wardrobes, and to the age, sex and anticipated growth rate of the child. The wardrobes selected reflect a reasonable representation of the kind of clothes that children wear at different ages. It has been assumed that heavier wear and tear occurs in relation to boys' trousers than to girls' clothes up to the teenage years.

66

6.4 Comparison of results

The study group constructed a detailed clothes list based on the York Family Budget Study which costed clothes for boys aged ten to twelve years. From this base the group constructed detailed lists for the other age groups. Table 6.1 shows the wardrobe for boys aged ten to twelve used by the Family Budget Unit, Bradshaw and Morgan, Murphy-Lawless. The final columns indicate the composite clothing list as decided for this study.

Table 6.1 Comparison of Wardrobes for a Boy Aged 10-12

Item	Family Budget Unit		Bradshaw & Morgan		Murphy-Lawless		Current Study	
	Quantity	Lifespan (years)	Quantity	Lifespan (years)	Quantity	Lifespan (years)	Quantity	Lifespan (years)
Anorak/coat	1	2	1	2	1	2	1	1
Summer Jacket	1	2	-	-	-	-	-	-
Raincoat	1	3	-	-	-	-	1	1
Tracksuit	1	2	-	-	-	-	1	1
Trousers	4	2	3	0.75	1	0.75	4	0.5
Jeans	2	2	-	-	2	0.75	1	1
School shirt	3	1	3	0.75	2	0.75	4	1
Other shirts	8	2	-	-	-	-	-	-
T shirts	7	2	2	0.75	2	1	4	1
Jumpers	9	2	2	1.5	2	1.5	2	2
Sweatshirt	2	2	1	1.5	1	1.5	1	1
Shorts	2	2	1	1.5	1	1	2	1
Swimming trunks	1	2	1	1.5	1	2	1	2
Underpants	9	2	6	0.75	6	2	6	1
Vests	4	2	2	1.5	2	1	2	1
Pyjamas	4	2	2	1.75	2	1	2	1
Dressing gown	1	2	1	2	1	2	1	2
Socks	17	2	6	0.75	6	0.75	6	1
Hat	2	3	-	-	-	-	-	-
Scarf	1	3	-	-	-	-	1	3
Gloves	1	3	1	2	1	2	1	2
Shoes	5	1	1	0.5	1	0.5	1	0.5
Runners	2	1	1	0.5	1	0.5	1	0.5
Slippers	1	1	-	-	-	-	1	1
Wellies	1	2	-	-	-	-	1	2

Household Budget Survey

The *Household Budget Survey* figures on average spending on children's clothing by family size are shown below (Figure 6.2). Since children's clothes are defined as clothes for those aged under fourteen, spending on clothes for older teenagers is likely to be subsumed under the figures for adult clothing in the *Household Budget Survey*. It is important to bear this in mind when considering costs for some family types as larger families are more likely to have teenage children. Clothes are occasional rather than regular purchases, therefore the sampling error will be larger than in the case of food spending. These factors may account in part for the change in the gradient as family size increases. It may reflect in part, economies of scale in passing on clothes from older to younger children, and also the likelihood that smaller families may have a higher per capita income and therefore buy higher priced more fashionable items.

Figure 6.2 Average Weekly Spending on Children's Clothes by Family Size, 1992 Prices

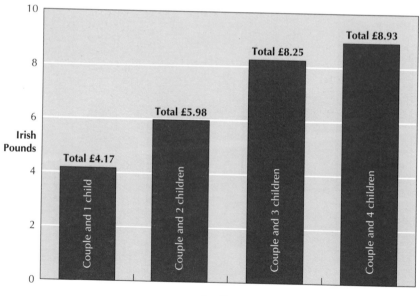

Source: Appendix C, Table C.7

It has already been noted that these figures are sensitive to the anticipated lifetimes of clothes. Clothes spending by one-child families in the *Household Budget Survey* (which consists of roughly half baby clothes) is of broadly the same order of magnitude as the cost of clothes for one child in the current study. However, the *Household Budget Survey* figures, even granted the caveats above, suggest that clothes spending per head falls significantly in larger families. Jo Murphy-Lawless's study (1992), based on subsamples of the same *Household Budget Survey*, shows similarly that clothing is one of the principal areas where poorer families cut back on expenditure, through using second-hand or passed on clothes or wearing clothes after they are worn out. Given the expense involved in purchasing clothing it would seem likely that larger families would be likely to pursue similar strategies.

6.5 Summary
- The weekly cost of clothing under the Basic Minimum Budget Standard ranges from £5.55 for a baby to £7.02 for a teenager over twelve years of age.
- The weekly cost of clothing does not increase consistently with age; costs fall in the pre-school years before rising consistently thereafter.
- The purchase of clothes for back to school, first communion and confirmation and other special occasions causes significant clustering of expenditure.
- The cost of clothing for girls' is consistently higher in each age group. This is despite the shorter lifespan of boys' clothing.

Chapter 7 - Education and Extra-Curricular Costs

7. Introduction

The educational costs for primary and secondary level schools under the Basic Minimum Budget standard are presented in Figure 7.1 below. In costing this section, information was used from studies undertaken by the National Parents' Council into school costs (National Parents' Council, 1990 and 1991), from the study of education costs by the PAUL Project in Limerick (1991), and from book lists obtained from individual schools.

Figure 7.1 Weekly Educational Costs for Primary and Secondary - Basic Minimum Standard, 1992

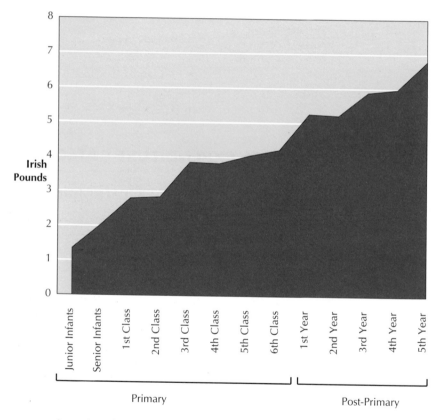

Source: Appendix C, Table C.8

72

7.1 Budgetary standards
Basic Minimum Budget standard
The main financial costs of education under a Basic Minimum Budget standard are textbooks[21], stationery (copybooks and pencils), equipment (rulers, rubbers and geometry sets), transport and school extras. School extras include the cost of extra-curricular activities and associated equipment, exam fees, school tours, school milk/drink (school lunches are covered under the food budget, Chapter 5[22]), and "voluntary" contributions towards school fundraising. School uniforms have already been costed into the clothing budget (Chapter 6).

Modest-but-Adequate Budget Standard
While recognising the importance of pre-school education, this item has not been included in the Basic Minimum Budget standard calculation. It has, however, been included under the Modest-but-Adequate standard. The cost of playgroup or pre-school participation would be around £6 a week for a playgroup over a 33- to 39-week term. Averaged out over the whole year, this is £4.15 a week.

7.2 Costing education: primary school costs
Textbooks and stationery
The study group costed textbooks for primary school pupils in 1991 in a Dublin primary school. The selected primary school, The Queen of Angels National School, serves a catchment area of mixed social class. While these costings did not include school stationery, an allowance was made for stationery expenses; £2 per year up to second class and £5.20 per year from third to sixth class.

The cost of textbooks and school stationery were not found to rise consistently each year. However a general trend towards increasing costs with age was apparent. It is estimated in the current study that textbooks and stationery would cost almost £27 in junior infant classes and up to £63 in the final years of primary school (Table 7.1). However, it is worth noting that the biggest increase in costs occurs in the transition from infant classes to first class.

---

[21] A limited supply of textbooks is available to children in primary, secondary and vocational schools under a grant-in-aid from the Department of Education. For further discussion of the free school-books scheme see Chapter 2 above.

[22] Light school meals may be made available to pupils who require them in schools in urban areas and in certain areas of the Gaeltacht. For further discussion of the free school meals scheme see Chapter 2 above.

Costings for textbooks and stationery in the current study are compared with the costing presented in the National Parents' Council (NPC)(1990) study of textbooks and stationery costings in a Tipperary National School. The costings from both the NPC study and the current study are brought to 1992 figures using the Consumer Price Index (Table 7.1). Differences in the costings are partially due to differences in the choice of textbooks.

Table 7.1 Annual Cost of Textbooks and Stationery, 1992

	National Parents' Council Costings (1990) 1992 Prices	Current Study (1991) 1992 Prices
Junior Infants	23.04	26.84
Senior Infants	24.66	24.03
1st Class	39.05	42.59
2nd Class	46.11	44.52
3rd Class	46.85	53.26
4th Class	52.73	51.57
5th Class	53.87	63.36
6th Class	47.51	62.41

If textbooks were not changed, there would be some scope for passing on such books to a younger brother or sister, but workbooks and arts and crafts materials would need to be bought separately for each child. At senior infant level, £13.05 of the cost estimated above relates to work materials which could not be passed down. By fifth class, in contrast, only £10 of the total cost refers to workbooks and materials. However, the study group considers that schools should be in a position to choose the most appropriate textbooks and that regular changes in textbooks are to be expected over time.

Extraneous costs of primary school

While textbooks and school stationery constitute the most obvious costs of educating children, extraneous expenditure also constitutes a significant proportion of education costs. These would include a school drink, transport, "voluntary" contributions and extra-curricular activities.

Children who live within walking or cycling distance of school, or who are eligible for free transport, will have no transport costs. For other children, transport costs may amount to £90 for a school year at primary level, and £96 a year at second level. School transport costs have not been included in the budgets compiled for the current study but of course such costs should be added for those children, mainly in rural areas, who need transport to school and are not eligible for free transport.

The cost of a basic school uniform, priced in a chainstore, has already been included in the clothing budget presented in Chapter 6 above. However, where a school nominates a particular make or supplier for the uniform it is likely to prove more expensive.

In relation to school bags there is already a strong relationship between quality and lifespan whereby older children with a heavier bookload will wear out their schoolbag more rapidly than will younger children. For the purpose of the current study it was estimated for infant classes that a £4.99 schoolbag would last two years; for first and second class, a £10 bag would last two years; for third and fourth class, a £15 bag would last two years; and for fifth and sixth class, a £15 bag would last two years. It was assumed that the cost of school lunches, other than drinks, had already been included in the cost of food presented in Chapter 5 above. School milk is costed at £4.50 per term per child which amounts to 25p per week when spread over a full year. In sixth class, there may be the additional cost of an entrance assessment for second level; this has been priced at £10.

In addition to the above costs many schools organise school tours. Primary school staff members estimate the annual costs of these tours as £4 for infants, and £7-£9 for first to sixth class pupils. A drama group visit to the school would cost £1.50 per pupil, and a trip to Croke Park for a football final, £1.50 per pupil. Extra pocket money/sweets or drinks are also likely to be required for the child on a school outing, probably costing 50p up to fourth class, and £1 for fifth and sixth classes.

The school also requests a "voluntary" contribution of £20 per family, and holds an annual raffle at a cost of £10 per family to augment school funds. The National Parents' Council study showed a national average for voluntary contributions over a sample of 371 schools of £10 per pupil, and up to an average of £13.90 per pupil in Dublin schools. An annual figure of £20 per child has been included in the present study to cover both voluntary donations and school raffles. These were considered by the study group to be real costs that parents face if their children are not to feel marginalised and so should be included.

As sport, music and other activities after school hours are often organised through schools, these have been included in the education budget. This heading is also intended to cover similar activities organised within the community rather than through the schools. It is felt that participation in such activities should form a natural part of a child's normal development, and therefore that allowance for the cost of one weekly activity from senior infants to second class, and of two weekly activities from third class onwards (eg football and scouts), would be reasonable. The allowance rate of £1 a week per activity seems to represent a fairly typical cost, although the true cost obviously would vary from one activity to another: this average cost works out at £39 per child per year in the junior classes, and £78 per child per year in the senior classes. The rough estimates made in respect of the cost of special clothes and equipment are calculated to average out at about £15 per child per year.

When the above additions are made to the base costs in Table 7.1 the total costs for primary level education rise significantly. In most classes the costs rise by over 200 per cent, and by as much as 300 per cent in Senior Infants. These additions to the base cost of primary education are presented in Table 7.2.

Table 7.2 Annual Cost of Educating a Child at Primary Level, 1992

	Textbooks Stationery	School Milk/Drink	School Bag	Voluntary Contribution	Visits, Tours & DramaGroup	Extra Curricular Activities	Sports Gear	Exam Fee	Total Yearly	Total Weekly
Junior Infants	26.84	13.50	2.50	20.00	7.50	-	-	-	70.34	1.35
Senior Infants	24.03	13.50	2.50	20.00	7.50	39.00	-	-	106.53	2.05
1st Class	42.59	13.50	5.00	20.00	10.50	39.00	15.00	-	145.59	2.80
2nd Class	44.52	13.50	5.00	20.00	10.50	39.00	15.00	-	147.52	2.84
3rd Class	53.26	13.50	7.50	20.00	13.00	78.00	15.00	-	200.26	3.85
4th Class	51.57	13.50	7.50	20.00	13.00	78.00	15.00	-	198.57	3.82
5th Class	63.36	13.50	7.50	20.00	13.00	78.00	15.00	-	210.36	4.05
6th Class	62.40	13.50	7.50	20.00	13.00	78.00	15.00	10.00	219.40	4.22

7.3 Costing education: post-primary school costs
Textbooks, stationery and equipment

For second level costs, the National Parents' Council (1991) report on schooling costs was examined and cross checked against the costs available for St Tiernan's School, a south Dublin community school serving a mixed catchment area. Since the costs associated with textbooks were comparable in both instances and since full equipment costs for St. Tiernan's were not available, it was decided to base the estimates for textbooks, stationery and equipment on the figures cited by the National Parents' Council, but with the following modifications. In the cost figures for textbooks, stationery and equipment it is assumed that a student takes Irish, English, maths, French, history, geography, science, religion and home economics to Junior Certificate level; and Irish, English, maths, chemistry, technical drawing, French and home economics to Leaving Certificate level. A different choice of subjects is likely to produce similar costs. As school texts and equipment vary from subject to subject, total costs will obviously be influenced by subject choice. In addition, practical subjects would have extra costs for materials and equipment; for example the National Parents' Council study assumed material costs for twenty classes of £3 per class in home economics for first and second year dropping down to £1 per class in third year. The study team felt that the latter represented a more realistic figure, so material costs for a child for all three years are taken as £1 per class or £20 over the full school year. Table 7.3 shows the costs of textbooks, stationery and equipment for each year of second level.

Table 7.3 Annual Cost of Textbooks, Stationery and Equipment, 1992

	Textbooks £	Stationery and Equipment £
1st year	99.05	31.37
2nd year	90.98	37.37
3rd year	91.89	31.82*
4th year	93.32	65.50
5th year	58.00	79.00

* As no costings were given for 3rd Year stationery requirements in the National Parents' Council (1991), an estimation of the costs are included.

Many post-primary textbooks will be used for an entire cycle particularly in the case of the two-year senior cycle. As a result, the cost of textbooks is considerably higher in the first year of a cycle (ie first year and fourth year) dropping in the later years.

Extraneous costs of post-primary school

As is the case with primary school costs many extraneous costs also arise in regard to second level education. Allowance has been made for these in the Basic Minimum Budget. A voluntary contribution to the school of £20 per pupil has been included for each year. Examination fees cover mock examinations, Junior and Leaving Certificate examinations and third level application fees. A cost of £12 is added for a school tour each year. It is assumed that two £20 schoolbags will last a pupil for the whole of the second cycle.

If a student takes a hot drink in school costing 20p a day, the cost over the school year works out at £33 in the year, or an extra 63p a week averaged over the whole year, and this is included in the total. It is assumed that school lunches, with the exception of a drink, have already been included in the main family food budget. The figures for school lunches given by the PAUL study (1991) show an average cost of school lunches at £2.74 a day, with a range from of from £1 to £6 daily for this age group, and the National Parents' Council costings at second level assume school lunches at £2 per school day per child.

As second level students have less free time than younger students during the school year, participation is assumed in only one organised sport or extra-curricular activity, costing £1 a week per pupil over a 33-week school year. Football has been taken for boys, and basketball for girls, as a guide to the costs although these inevitably will vary from one sport or activity to another. It is assumed over the five-year cycle that a boy will have two pairs of football boots, two football strips, and two gear bags; and that girls will have two pairs of basketball boots, two strips, and two gear bags. For both boys and girls, this gear is assumed to cost about £17 a year. Under the heading pocket money and transport, £1 expenditure per week over a 33-week school year has been included in the estimates for personal busfares for teenagers, and it is assumed that this amount will also cover the cost of transport for such occasions as away matches.

Second level students are likely to make educational visits to the theatre to see the prescribed play, to the Young Scientist Exhibition and to such venues as career days and open days. The cost for students in rural areas is likely to be higher in this respect in view of extra transport costs or an overnight stay in Dublin. We suggest that £20 for Junior Certificate and £30 for Leaving Certificate pupils would reasonably cover such admission and transport costs.

When the costs outlined in Table 7.3 are adjusted to take account of the above additions, the total annual and weekly costs arrived at are as outlined in Table 7.4. As with the costs of primary level education the costs per week of second level education increased significantly when extraneous costs were taken into account. The final costs ranged from £5.26 in first year to £6.80 in the final year of secondary school.

Table 7.4 Annual Cost of Educating a Child at Second Level, 1992

	Textbooks Stationery	School Milk/Drink	School Bag	Voluntary Contribution	Educational Visits & Tours	Extra Curricular Activities	Sports Gear	Exam Fee	Total Yearly	Total Weekly
1st Yr	130.42	33.00	8.00	20.00	32.00	33.00	17.00	-	273.42	5.26
2nd Yr	128.35	33.00	8.00	20.00	32.00	33.00	17.00	-	271.35	5.22
3rd Yr	123.71	33.00	8.00	20.00	32.00	33.00	17.00	39.50	306.21	5.89
4th Yr	157.82	33.00	8.00	20.00	42.00	33.00	17.00	-	310.82	5.98
5th Yr	137.00	33.00	8.00	20.00	42.00	33.00	17.00	63.50	353.50	6.80

7.4 Comparison of results

Because education expenditure, as defined in the current study, comes under different headings in the *Household Budget Survey*, it is not easy to obtain comparable figures. For textbooks, the *1987 Household Budget Survey* figures show average household spending rising from 47p a week at the early school stage, to £1.20 a week where the eldest child is aged fifteen to nineteen. As has already been noted, in addition to the cost of textbooks, allowance is also made in the current study for the cost of extra-curricular activities such as sport, educational visits and donations to fund-raising activities.

7.5 Summary

- The weekly cost of primary education under the Basic Minimum Budget standard ranges from £1.35 for a child in junior infants to £6.80 for a teenager in the final year of secondary school.
- The weekly cost of education rises as the child move up through the education system.
- Extraneous costs such as educational tours, extra-curricular activities, exam fees and school drinks account for a significant proportion of the costs associated with education.

COSTING INDIVIDUAL EXPENDITURE CATEGORIES

Chapter 8 - Personal Care and Medical Costs

8. Introduction

This chapter looks at personal care costs and the cost of medical care. These costs are directly related to the number of children, with no real expectation of economies of scale. Under personal care, the cost of baby-sitting younger children to allow parents an occasional night out is also estimated. This is not included in the summary figure estimated for the Basic Minimum Budget standard but is included in the Modest-but-Adequate Budget standard. A summary budget of personal care and medical care costs is presented in Figure 8.1.

Figure 8.1 Weekly Cost of Personal Care - Basic Minimum Standard, 1992

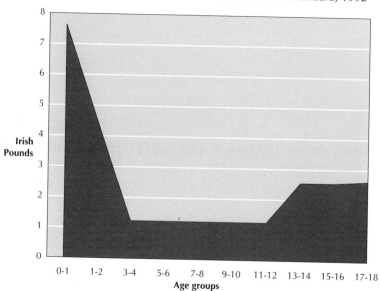

Source: Appendix C, Table C.9

8.1 Budgetary standards
Basic Minimum Budget Standard

The categories that make up these personal care costs under the Basic Minimum Budget standard are toiletries, nappies, haircare, a first-aid kit, and washing powder. Dental care is also included for children aged thirteen to eighteen. Dental care for children of primary school age is provided free. Medical costs are not included in the estimates for the Basic Minimum Budget standard since it is assumed that low-income families will have medical cards which will be applicable to their children. Table 8.1 below, gives a breakdown of the various weekly costs in each category according to age.

Table 8.1 Itemised Weekly Cost of Personal Care - Basic Minimum Standard, 1992

Age/ Items	under 1 £	1-2 £	3-4 £	5-6 £	7-8 £	9-10 £	11-12 £	13-14 £	15-16 £	17-18 £
Toiletries	1.24	1.02	0.46	0.46	0.46	0.46	0.46	1.29	1.29	1.40
Nappies	6.01	3.02								
Haircare			0.39	0.39	0.39	0.39	0.39	0.39	0.39	0.39
First-aid kit	0.04	0.04	0.04	0.04	0.04	0.04	0.04	0.04	0.04	0.04
Dental Care								0.44	0.44	0.44
Washing Powder	0.35	0.35	0.35	0.35	0.35	0.35	0.35	0.35	0.35	0.35
Total	**7.64**	**4.43**	**1.24**	**1.24**	**1.24**	**1.24**	**1.24**	**2.51**	**2.51**	**2.62**

Modest-but-Adequate Budget standard
Medical costs, excluded from the Basic Minimum Budget, are included in the Modest-but-Adequate Budget standard. These costs would add, on average, 38p per week to the budget. Baby-sitting costs, allowing parents a night out once a fortnight, would add a further £2.50 per week to the Modest-but-Adequate Budget for children up to the age of twelve. This latter cost, of course, will be affected by the presence of older children, and by the availability of relatives to babysit.

Table 8.2 Weekly Cost of Personal Care and Medical Care - Modest-but-Adequate, 1992

Age/ Items	under 1 £	1-2 £	3-4 £	5-6 £	7-8 £	9-10 £	11-12 £	13-14 £	15-16 £	17-18 £
Toiletries	1.24	1.02	0.46	0.46	0.46	0.46	0.46	1.29	1.29	1.40
Nappies	6.01	3.02								
Haircare			0.39	0.39	0.39	0.39	0.39	0.39	0.39	0.39
First-aid kit	0.04	0.04	0.04	0.04	0.04	0.04	0.04	0.04	0.04	0.04
Dental Care								0.44	0.44	0.44
Washing Powder	0.35	0.35	0.35	0.35	0.35	0.35	0.35	0.35	0.35	0.35
Medical Costs	0.46	0.46	0.46	0.30	0.30	0.30	0.30	0.30	0.38	0.38
Baby-sitting	2.50	2.50	2.50	2.50	2.50	2.50	2.50	-	-	-
Total	**10.60**	**7.39**	**4.20**	**4.04**	**4.04**	**4.04**	**4.04**	**2.81**	**2.89**	**3.00**

8.2 Costing personal care and medical care
Baby Nappies
Disposable nappies were considered by the study group to now be the norm for babies. If cloth nappies were to be used there would be alternative costs with washing which some studies have shown can be almost as expensive as using disposable nappies. Therefore it is assumed for the purpose of this study that babies use disposable nappies. The toilet training of babies generally commences at about the age of eighteen months and nappies are usually used at night until age two and a half years. It is assumed for the purpose of this study that babies use seven nappies per day up to six months; five nappies per day from six to eighteen months; and then one night-grade nappy until aged two and a half years. The costs involved are outlined in Table 8.3 below.

Table 8.3 Cost of Nappies - Basic Minimum Standard, 1992

Size	Babys Age Months	Price £	Weekly Number	Weekly Cost £
Newborn	0-3 mths	3.49 for 28	49	6.11
Mini	3-6 mths	7.89 for 60	49	6.44
Midi	6-12 mths	7.89 for 48	35	5.75
Maxi	12-18 mths	13.99 for 84	35	5.83
Junior	18-30 mths	7.89 for 34	7	1.62

Source: Crazy Prices, Chainstore.

This gives an average weekly cost for nappies of £6.01 for the zero to one year age range and £3.02 for the one to two year age range.

Baby toiletries
The basic budget estimates also include baby toiletries such as nappy cream, baby wipes and baby lotions. It is assumed that a pack of eighty baby wipes (£1.89), and a 300ml bottle of baby lotion (£1.73) will last four weeks for babies aged up to six months, and twice as long for older babies. It is also

assumed that, on average, one jar of nappy cream (£2.89), and one bottle of baby shampoo (£1.99) is used every two months. Total baby toiletries under these assumptions come to £1.46 a week for babies up to six months and £1.02 for the older babies (Table 8.4).

Table 8.4 Cost of Baby Toiletries - Basic Minimum Standard, 1992

Item	Unit Price £	Annual cost £	Weekly cost £
Babies aged 0-6 months			
Baby wipes	1.89	24.57	0.47
Baby lotion	1.73	22.49	0.43
Nappy cream	2.89	17.34	0.33
Baby shampoo	1.99	11.94	0.23
Total cost for babies aged 0-6 months		**76.34**	**1.46**
Babies over 6 months			
Baby wipes	1.89	12.29	0.24
Baby lotion	1.73	11.25	0.22
Nappy cream	2.89	17.34	0.33
Baby shampoo	1.99	11.94	0.23
Total cost for babies aged over 6 months		**52.82**	**1.02**

Toiletries

The items costed under this heading are toilet tissue, soap, shampoo, and toothpaste. For children aged three to twelve, the list of toiletries compiled by the Family Budget Unit in York is used i.e. annual consumption per head of four bars of soap, three tubes of toothpaste and 1.5 litres of shampoo. In addition, usage is assumed of one roll of toilet tissue per person per week and of a new toothbrush every nine months. Allowance is also made for a wider range and for the heavier use of toiletries by adolescents (see Table 8.5).

Table 8.5 Cost of Toiletries - Basic Minimum Standard, 1992

Item	Unit Price £	Annual cost £	Weekly cost £
Soap	0.36	1.46	0.03
Toothpaste	0.79	2.37	0.05
Shampoo	0.78	1.17	0.02
Toilet Tissue	0.35	18.43	0.35
Toothbrush	0.54	0.73	0.01
Total for children aged 3-12 years		**24.16**	**0.46**
Additional for Teenage girls			
Deodorant	1.51	18.12	0.35
Shower gel	1.19	14.28	0.28
Tampax	1.73	20.80	0.40
Sub total		53.20	1.03
Total for Teenage girls		**77.36**	**1.49**
Additional for Teenage boys aged 13-16			
Deodorant	1.51	18.12	0.35
Shower gel	1.19	14.28	0.28
Sub total		32.40	0.63
Total for Teenage boy aged 13-16		**56.56**	**1.09**
Additional for Teenage boys aged 17-18			
Deodorant	1.51	18.12	0.35
Shower gel	1.19	14.28	0.28
Razor blades and shaving cream	0.91	10.92	0.21
Sub total		43.32	0.84
Total for Teenage boys aged 17-18		**67.48**	**1.30**

Source: Crazy Prices, Chainstore

Heavier use of toiletries such as deodorants and shower gel, sanitary protection for girls, and razors for older boys are included in the Basic Minimum Budget. Deodorant priced at 35p per week for both boys and girls, and shower gel at 28p per week bring the cost of toiletries for adolescents to £1.09. For teenage boys of seventeen to eighteen the cost of razor blades and shaving cream is estimated at 21p per week which takes the total cost of toiletries for boys in this age group to £1.30 per week. For teenage girls of thirteen to eighteen the use of 25 Tampax a month has been estimated at 40p per week which takes their total to £1.49. Any cosmetics over and above this list, are assumed to come from the pocket money budget.

Haircare
Provision has been made for a haircut costing £5 once every three months for children over two years of age. This works out at 39p per week.

Washing powder
The washing powder budget from the York Family Budget Unit is based on the recommendations of the consumer journal *Which?* They suggest that 175g of automatic washing powder is used per wash load. Each child will therefore require about 350g a week in washing powder. The average weekly cost of 350g of washing power is about 35p.

First-aid kit
Over and above prescribed medicines, families are likely to keep a store of proprietary medicines, such as bandages. The first-aid kit for a year suggested by the Family Budget Unit in York for a family with two children, is a junior cough mixture of 125ml and junior paracetamol of 70ml in addition to adult home remedies. This first-aid kit would work out at 4p a week per child.

Dental care
Dental care for children of primary school age is available free of charge but teenagers at second level must pay. The cost will vary depending on the problems - for example, a course of orthodontic care could cost up to £2,000. One check-up dental visit per year is costed into the Basic Minimum Budget estimate for second level students at £15 and two fillings at £20 each over the five years of second level education. Dental care costs on this basis would average £23 a year, or 44p a week for children aged over twelve.

Medical care

Medical costs have not been included in the Basic Minimum Budget as it is assumed that most families on low-income will be entitled to free medical care. A medical care budget has been costed for the Modest-but-Adequate Budget based on the average number of visits to the doctor by children of different ages which has been recorded in the *1987 Household Budget Survey* (1989, Table 1A :26). Children aged up to four make an average of 1.25 visits a year, those aged five to fourteen, 0.7 visits a year, and aged fifteen to twenty, 0.9 visits a year. General Practitioners (GPs) visits have been priced at £15 each, and also included is a course of antibiotics for each visit to the doctor. Paediatric amoxycillin would cost £4 for a course, and regular amoxycillin, £7 a course. On this basis the average weekly cost of medical care works out at 46p for a child aged up to four, 30p for a child aged five to fourteen, and 38p for age fifteen to eighteen.

Table 8.6 Cost of Medical Care - Modest-but-Adequate Standard, 1992

Age	GP Visits per year	Cost per Visit £	Cost of medicine per visit £	Yearly Cost £	Weekly Cost £
0-4 years	1.25	15.00	4.00	23.75	0.46
5-14 years	0.70	15.00	7.00	15.40	0.30
15-20 years	0.90	15.00	7.00	19.80	0.38
Average				**58.95**	**0.38**

Source: *1987 Household Budget Survey*, (1989)

These costings for medical care assume that neither the family nor the child possesses a medical card. Medical card holders face no charges for GP visits nor for prescribed medicines which appear on the official list. No allowance has been made in the budgets for an additional voluntary health insurance premium for children, since hospital treatment is available to all in public wards.

The cost figures assume average good health. For example, medical care for an asthmatic child could cost considerably more, with a preventive inhaler such as Intal costing about £25 a month. No outpatient or inpatient hospital charges have been included for children, nor has any figure for glasses, worn by about 17 per cent of ten-year-olds, and 28 per cent of fifteen-year-olds (information obtained from Optical Department, Kevin Street College of Technology).

Spending under the medical care heading is averaged out over the year to give a weekly figure. Obviously, medical costs will be clustered when illness occurs and will be nil at other times. An infection that affects the whole family would leave many parents paying considerably more in a given week than the average figures stated above.

Baby-sitting
In the case of young children, parents may have to pay a baby-sitter in order to arrange a night out. A typical rate for a baby-sitter would be £5 a night up to midnight, and £10 for a later night. A night out for parents once a fortnight would thus work out at an average of £2.50 a week in baby-sitting costs, whether for one or more children. Children may need a baby-sitter at night up to age ten or twelve. If there are older children or other relatives available to mind younger ones, parents may not always need a paid baby-sitter. The cost of baby-sitting is not included in the Basic Minimum Budget but has been included in the Modest-but-Adequate Budget standard.

Childcare
No costs have been included for childcare expenditure for parents going out to work, nor for income forgone by a parent who works full time in the home, since this report deals only with the direct costs incurred in the rearing of children.

8.3 Comparison of results
The *1987 Household Budget Survey* confirms the finding in this study that families with very young children spend a lot of money on baby toiletries. This imbalance in costs occurs because baby toiletries will consume a large proportion of the personal care budget if babies are to be kept scrupulously clean and free from nappy rash. While the average household in the *1987 Household Budget Survey* spent 83p a week on toiletries, families with pre-school children were spending £3.40 a week on these items and families in the survey with one child, who were mainly families with a young baby or toddler, were spending on average £2.36 a week on toiletries. The

Household Budget Survey does not, however, specify nappies as an item in the list of toiletries.

No comparable figures are available for health care costs applicable to families in the UK since health care is available free of charge under the National Health Service.

8.4 Summary

- Under the Basic Minimum Budget the average weekly costs associated with personal care range from £7.64 for children aged under one year to £2.62 for teenagers aged seventeen to eighteen years.
- The Modest-but-Adequate Budget standard allows for medical care costs and baby-sitting costs in addition to the costings outlined in the Basic Minimum Budget. This gives a cost range of £10.60 per week for children aged under one year old to £3.00 per week for seventeen to eighteen year olds.
- Personal care costs decline sharply once children are toilet trained. They remain stable between ages three and twelve years and rise slightly higher during the teenage years due to the greater personal care requirements of teenagers.
- Differences in the personal care costs of boys and girls only emerge in the teenage years with girls costing on average 28p per week more in these years.
- Medical care under the Modest-but-Adequate Budget standard costs on average 38p per week.

COSTING INDIVIDUAL EXPENDITURE CATEGORIES

Chapter 9 - Housing

9. Introduction

The focus of the budget standard is on the marginal cost of children. As discussed below, rarely would an extra child result in extra housing costs. Therefore, no figure for additional housing cost has been included in the overall budgets.

9.1 Bedroom space

The marginal cost of housing in respect of children can be evaluated by looking at the extra bedrooms needed for additional children. For example, the first child would increase the space needed from one bedroom to two. A second child of the same sex can be expected to share the bedroom; a child of opposite sex would need an extra bedroom. As families grow, additional bedroom space may be needed. A standard three-bedroom house can accommodate three to four children sleeping in ordinary beds, possibly more if bunk beds are used. The most common types of family home in Ireland are three- or four-bedroom houses, and 94 per cent of Irish families have four or fewer children (Department of Social Welfare, 1991a, Table C:18). At a basic living standard, an additional bedroom would only be strictly necessary for the larger families. The private housing market in Ireland indicates that purchasers contemplating a family usually opt for at least three-bedroom housing from the outset.

9.2 Tenure

The cost of accommodation for most Irish families is not consistently related to house size. Rather, housing costs vary substantially according to location, tenure, and if owner-occupied, the length of time since purchase. For the dominant tenure, owner-occupied housing, the length of time since purchase is a major factor in the current cost. Because families with older children would typically have bought their homes at an earlier time and for a lower price than families with younger children, the average spending on housing declines steadily with later stages of the life cycle. Moreover, families with children are more likely to buy their homes with a mortgage, rent from a local authority or rent privately, than to be outright owners. The *1987 Household Budget Survey* reported that the cost of housing at the pre-family stage was on average £49 per week, falling to £29 a week at the early school stage (*1987 Household Budget Survey*, 1989: Table 9: 128-129). Average spending on housing also falls steadily with increases in family size, again probably reflecting the fact that larger families purchased at an earlier date than small families which were still in the first stages of family formation.

Figure 9.1 Housing Tenure in Ireland

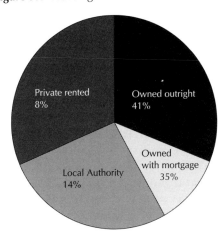

Source: Appendix C, Table C.10

9.3 Private rented housing

Private rented housing caters largely for single people, and relatively few families with children are in the private rental market. For those who are, the marginal cost of having the first child will inevitably be considerably higher.

For those in private rented housing, the difference in the costs of the extra space needed for children is more clearcut. A single room would cost about £30 a week to rent in the Dublin area, a second bedroom would be likely to cost an extra £20-£30 a week. A three-bedroom house would be likely to cost £300-£400 a month to rent, depending on location.

9.4 Local authority housing

Local authority rents are assessed on the income of the principal earner, and are not related to the size of the accommodation. Families with similar incomes pay the same rent whether for a two-bedroomed flat or a four-bedroomed house. In principal, rents should not vary with the size of the family. In practice, the rent formula used means that rents may increase for tenants on welfare as welfare payments rise with family size.

9.5 Comparison of results

It was decided not to include any figure for housing costs in the budget totals given for children. Conniffe and Keogh (1988:79) similarly excluded housing from their estimates of equivalence scales for children on the grounds that "there is little evidence, overall, for any contribution of the presence of a child to housing (expenditure)."

9.6 Summary

- The proportion of accommodation costs attributable to children is difficult to establish and therefore has not been included in the budgets presented in this study.
- The cost of accommodation is not consistently related to the size of the accommodation, because costs vary according to location and tenure and, if owner occupied, the length of time since purchase.
- In the private rented sector in Dublin the cost of an extra room for a child would be likely to amount to between £20 and £30 per week.
- Local authority rents are not, in principle, related to the size of the accommodation although increases in family size may, vis a vis increased social welfare payments, have some adverse effects on the levels of rental assessment.

COSTING INDIVIDUAL EXPENDITURE CATEGORIES

Chapter 10 - Fuel

10. Introduction
In calculating the fuel budget for children only, the estimated cost of lighting, hot water and clothes washing are included. No figure has been included for the child's share of family heating costs or for heating additional space for children.

10.1 Budgetary standards
Basic Minimum Budget Standard
The estimated weekly fuel budgets for children are shown in Table 10.1. The main variable cost item is water heating for baths and showers.

Table 10.1 Weekly Fuel Budgets for Children - Basic Minimum Budget

Fuel	Younger children (0-12) £	Teenagers (13-18) £
Heating	nil	nil
Light	0.05	0.10
Water heating	0.38	0.57
Washing Machine	0.13	0.13
Total	**0.56**	**0.80**

Washing machine
The figures in Table 10.2 below, are estimates of washloads per child. These are drawn from Purchase, Berning and Lyng (1982). The Electricity Supply Board (ESB) estimates that the average family uses six units of electricity per week for washing clothes, with one unit of electricity costing 7.14p. Therefore, if a child necessitates an extra 0.9 to 2.8 washloads a week over and above the required washes for a couple, the energy cost of clothes washing for a child works out at 7p-20p per child per week or an average sum of 13p per week per child.

Table 10.2 Clothes Washing by Family Size, 1992

No of Children	Washing loads	Extra load per child
0	4.3	-
1	7.1	2.8
2	9.8	2.7
3	11.4	1.6
4-6	14.1	0.9 - 2.7
Average	**9.9**	

Source: Purchase, Berning & Lyng (1982).

Hot water

An average bath requires about fifteen gallons of water. Four units of electricity are necessary to heat this volume of water. It is assumed that a shower uses approximately one third as much hot water (five gallons). Two baths per child would cost about 57p a week; one bath and one shower, about 38p a week. For teenagers, it is considered that baths or showers would be more frequent, perhaps an average of one bath and three showers a week, costing about 57p a week.

Lighting

Extra lighting at two hours a day from a 100w bulb would work out at 1.4 units a week, ie about 10p a week for older children. Because younger children go to bed earlier, half of this amount, ie 5p a week, is allowed for this age group.

10.2 Comparison of results

The two most common forms of heating in Irish homes are solid fuel central heating and open fires. The *Household Budget Survey* figures for solid fuel purchases by family size show no consistent pattern. Indeed if anything, a slight decrease with larger family size is evident. By stage of family cycle, the *1987 Household Budget Survey* shows average weekly spending on solid fuel rising by about £1.50 a week from the pre-family to the pre-school stage, with only marginal increases thereafter as the family moves through the later stages of child-rearing.

Families with children at home will require more heating than families where nobody is at home during normal working hours. However, it is not clear that children at home involve additional heating costs over and above the cost of heating the home for the mother or other caregiver. In many families, the norm appears to be to heat one or two rooms downstairs, either the kitchen alone or the kitchen and another room in which children can play. It is difficult to assess in what proportion of homes separate rooms are heated for teenagers doing homework. The cost of fuel is an important economic factor which may limit the number of rooms being heated.

Heating a bedroom for study for two hours a night with a 1kw electric fire, five nights a week, six months of the year, would cost on average an extra 40p a week. An extra room for study may be shared by two to three children. Since there is no clear evidence of the precise additional cost that could be allocated to each child or additional child, no extra amount is included for heating in the current study.

The *Household Budget Survey* figures suggest that on average the additional fuel costs for children constitute a fraction of total heating costs. They also show that average fuel costs rise over the family cycle, reflecting larger families at later stages and indicating the extra costs of baths, clothes washing and the heating of extra rooms as children get older.

Table 10.3 Average Weekly Fuel Spending by Family Size

Family Size	Fuel spending £
Couple	14.81
Couple with 1 child	14.27
Couple with 2 children	15.54
Couple with 3 children	16.72
Couple with 4+ children	16.78

Source: *Household Budget Survey*, updated by Consumer Price Index to 1992 prices

10.3 Summary

- The weekly fuel costs attributable to children range from 58p for children aged up to twelve years to 82p for teenagers.
- Fuel costs include use of the washing machine, water heating for baths and showers, and lighting.
- Water heating for baths and showers accounts for the largest proportion of the fuel budget for a child.
- Since it is difficult to establish the proportional heating consumption of children no amount has been included in this respect in the budget for children.

Chapter 11 - Household Durables

11. Introduction

With regard to household durables this study looks primarily at the household items directly related to children - the furnishing of a child's bedroom, bedclothes and the seating, crockery and cutlery used by additional family members. In addition, there would be further wear and tear on items used by the whole family, eg the washing machine, vacuum cleaner, iron, furniture and floor coverings, due to extra numbers. In practice, some of these items would need to be replaced immediately as they wore out, eg the washing machine, while replacement could be postponed for longer in the case of shabby carpets or furniture.

A stocklist of household durable items was drawn up, with estimated lifespans. Where a child would have outgrown an item, eg a cot, there will be assumed economies of scale in the passing on of this article to other children.

Table 11.1 Household Durables - Basic Minimum Standard, 1992

Age	under 1 £	1-2 £	3-4 £	5-6 £	7-8 £	9-10 £	11-12 £	13-14 £	15-16 £	17-18 £
Cost	1.86	1.86	0.94	0.94	0.94	0.94	0.94	0.94	0.94	0.94

11.1 Budgetary standards
Basic Minimum Budget Standard
The lifespan of different household durable items has been estimated for the Basic Minimum Budget standard, and an average weekly cost thus calculated as shown in Table 11.1 above. International studies consulted provide widely varying guidelines as to useful lifespan and, in line with other items, find that cheap furniture or furnishings tend to wear out sooner. The lifespans outlined in these studies were examined in the context of the discussions with the panel of mothers. This identified, for example, their experience that beds would need to be replaced at least once in a child's lifetime.

11.2 Costing household durables
Baby equipment
The study group constructed a stocklist of baby equipment as none of the studies examined had contained such figures. The items selected were priced in

Roches Stores, Dublin, with additional pricing for smaller items in a local pharmacy. Most of the selected items would be used by at least two successive children but, depending on wear, some will need replacing for a third or fourth child. In addition, some baby equipment may be passed on by extended family members. The value a family might obtain from baby equipment is likely to depend largely on how children are spaced in a family - whether the family will need two cots, or will need a double buggy. The wear and tear on prams and buggies is likely to be much heavier for families without a car.

The weekly cost of baby equipment has been calculated based on the purchase price divided by 104 (ie spread over the weeks of two years of babyhood) and also based on the full lifetime of the different items. These represent the costs for a first child, or a third or fourth child where the equipment has worn out. While, on average, most of the items could be expected to last about five years, it would be expected that on the arrival of a third child a family would need to replace on average half of the items. The full list of items, along with prices and weekly costs are outlined in Table 11.2

Table 11.2 Household Durables for 0-2-Year-Olds - Basic Minimum Standard, 1992

Item	Quantity of item	Lifetime	Price £	Weekly cost over 2 years £	Weekly cost over lifetime £
Cot	1	5 years	91.95	0.88	0.35
Cot mattress	1	5 years	13.95	0.13	0.05
Cot sheets	6	3 years	5.95	0.17	0.11
Blankets	4	5 years	5.95	0.23	0.09
Pram	1	10 years	225.00	2.16	0.43
Pram sheets	4	5 years	3.95	0.30	0.12
Pram mattress	1	2 years	4.25	0.04	0.04
Buggy	1	5 years	48.00	0.46	0.18
Baby chair	1	5 years	16.00	0.15	0.06
High chair	1	10 years	49.95	0.48	0.10
Car seat	1	10 years	65.00	0.63	0.13
Steriliser	1	5 years	9.15	0.09	0.04
Bottles	4	2 years	1.35	0.05	0.05
Bath	1	5 years	8.50	0.08	0.03
Changing mat	1	5 years	7.45	0.07	0.03
Potty	1	5 years	3.85	0.04	0.02
Total				**5.96**	**1.83**

Sources: Roches Stores, local pharmacy.

The average weekly cost of these items for a first baby, if they depreciate over a two-year period, would work out at £5.96 per week. Most of these items could be passed on to a second child; some items would need renewing for a third child. The average weekly cost, taking depreciation into account, works out at £1.83 per week.

Household durables for the 3-18 year age range
Table 11.3 lists basic household equipment required by older children, again looking at the extras to be provided in a family with children. The lifespans of household durables used by the York Family Budget Unit for a family with two children were considered to be reasonable by the study group undertaking the current report, and have been used to construct Table 11.3.

Table 11.3 Household Durables for 3-18 Year Olds - Basic Minimum Standard, 1992

Item	Quantity	Lifetime*	Price £	Weekly cost £
Bed	1	15 yrs	99.00	0.12
Chest of drawers	1	20 yrs	40.00	0.04
Wardrobe	1	20 yrs	119.00	0.11
Shelves	1	20 yrs	40.00	0.04
Sheets	4	5 yrs	7.50	0.12
Duvet	1	8 yrs	25.95	0.06
Duvet cover/Pillow set	2	8 yrs	14.95	0.07
Pillows	2	8 yrs	9.95	0.05
Bedroom carpet	12 sq. yrds	7 yrs	47.40**	0.13
Bedroom curtains (lined)	1 pair	8 yrs	27.00	0.06
Bath towel	1	8 yrs	10.95	0.03
Hand towel	1	8 yrs	3.25	0.01
Share of suite	20% 3 pce suite	15 yrs	600.00	0.15
Kitchen chair	1	15 yrs	25.00	0.03
Crockery	1 setting	10 yrs	4.19	0.01
Cutlery		25 yrs	4.00	0.01
Total				**0.94**

Sources: Forsye and Forsye, Capel St; Protea Furniture, Capel St.; Roches Stores, Nutgrove; Penneys, Nutgrove; McGowan Flooring; Discount Curtains, Finglas.
*   Lifespans of household durables based on the York Family Budget Unit estimates.
**   Bedroom carpet priced at £3.95 per sq. yard.

There would be some modest economies in furniture costs for a second child sharing a bedroom. The same wardrobe, floor covering and curtains would probably suffice so that the marginal cost of a second child in the same bedroom would be about 75p per week, or about 20p a week less than the cost of the first child in this respect.

11.3 Comparison of results

Household Budget Survey figures analysed by stages in the family cycle show that the major buying of household durables takes place in the pre-family stage. This is as would be expected given that most household items are used by adults irrespective of whether they have children or not. Furniture and other durable purchases by family size show an increase from an average of £9.88 a week for couples with one child, to £10.84 a week for couples with two children, to £12.13 a week in families with three children. Spending on durables, since it is so infrequent, is subject to substantial sampling error, and differences in the averages could reflect this reality as much as underlying differences in spending patterns.

11.4 Summary

- The cost of household durables under the Basic Minimum Budget standard amounts to £1.86 per week for children aged under two years and to 94p per week for children aged over two years.

Chapter 12 - Toys and Presents

12. Introduction

Books and toys were not regarded as luxuries since play activities constitute an important aspect of a child's healthy developmental needs. For this reason an allowance for spending on toys and presents has been allocated under both the Basic Minimum Budget standard and the Modest-but-Adequate Budget standard.

12.1 Budgetary standards

Basic Minimum Budget Standard

The *Household Budget Survey* shows that households with pre-school and early school-going children spend about £1.60 a week on toys. Parents appear to spend to a target budget rather than pricing individual items, this is the approach chosen for toys and presents in this study. In larger families, parents would generally have less money to spend per child. More durable toys like tricycles could be passed down from one child to the next and toys, books and games could be shared by the whole family. For the Basic Minimum Budget, it is estimated that between Christmas, birthday, and other seasonal celebrations, parents will spend £40 in a year on each child. The study group considered this to be a modest sum, and believed that many parents would be likely to spend more. Forty pounds per annum per child averages out at 77p per week per child. This would allow, for example, a £20 present for Christmas, a £10 present for a birthday, and £10 to cover a birthday party together with other seasonal celebrations such as Easter and Halloween, as well as the cost of other toys or books bought throughout the year.

Modest-but-Adequate Budget standard

For the Modest-but-Adequate Budget standard twice the spending under the Basic Minimum Budget is allowed: £80 per annum, or an average of £1.54 a week, for toys and presents.

12.2 Costing toys and presents

Table 12.1 prices a selection of toys to give an idea of what could be afforded within that annual budget. The budget would cover, for example, the purchase of a teddy, three picture books, and a Fisher Price toy house for a one-year-old; alternatively a toddler bicycle, and a selection of toy cars for a toddler could be purchased. An older child could be given a toy checkout for Christmas, together with a Sindy doll and a couple of books for her birthday. Teenagers could get clothes, sports goods, or music tapes. Under this budget, a new bicycle for a ten to twelve year old would take four years to buy, allowing for no other presents during that period of time.

Table 12.1 Cost of a Selection of Toys, 1992

	£	
Bicycle for 10-year-old	160.00	
Junior bicycle with stabilisers	54.95	
Toddler sit-in car	39.95	
Toddler bicycle	29.95	
Fisher Price house	22.95	
Playschool buggy	19.99	
Lego castle, medium	19.99	
Casdon Checkout	17.95	
Popstar Sindy Doll	8.99	
Chess set	5.99	
Teddy	4.99	
Duplo	3.99-17.99	
Picture Puffin/Puffin book	3.30-4.50	
500 piece jigsaw	3.49	
Toy cars	0.99-2.49	

Source: Banba Toys, Mary St, Dublin; Easons, Dublin; Bike shop, Nutgrove.

From the discussions with the panel of mothers, it was clear that parents who cannot afford outings, treats or a holiday for their children throughout the year, make extra efforts to give them what they want for Christmas, and could spend considerably more than the levels of expenditure delineated in this budget.

12.3 Summary

- A flat rate of 77p per week (or £40 per annum) is allowed for spending on toys and presents under the Basic Minimum Budget.
- It is estimated that twice the Basic Minimum spending will be spent under the Modest-but-Adequate Budget: £80 per annum or £1.54 per week.

Chapter 13 - Treats and Pocket Money

13. Introduction

Treats and pocket money have been regarded as interdependent for the purposes of this study - younger children may be bought sweets and drinks by their parents and older children will receive pocket money out of which they themselves will buy sweets, ice-cream, and crisps. Teenagers may fund fashion clothing, cosmetics, music, or discos from their pocket money. The weekly cost of pocket money and treats under the Basic Minimum Budget is shown for the different age groups in Figure 13.1.

Figure 13.1 Weekly Cost of Pocket Money and Treats

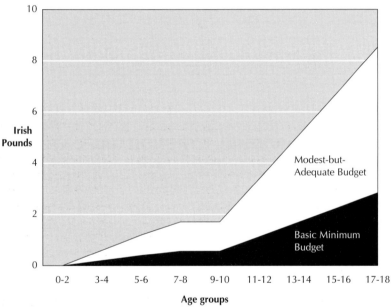

Source: Table 13.1 & Table 13.2

13.1 Budgetary standards
Basic Minimum Budget standard

Spending on pocket money and treats depends on how these items of expenditure are organised within individual households. Some parents give regular pocket money from which the children budget, some buy regular treats, some pay for individual outings and items as they arise, so that the parents may be recorded as spending on items such as entertainment, sweets or comics, rather than on pocket money.

112

Table 13.1 Weekly Cost of Pocket Money and Treats - Basic Minimum Standard, 1992

Age	Pocket money	Double pocket money for Summer*	Sweets	Total*
	£	£	£	£
0-2	-	-	-	-
3-4	-	-	0.20	0.20
5-6	-	-	0.40	0.40
7-8	0.50	0.07	-	0.57
9-10	0.50	0.07	-	0.57
11-12	1.00	0.13	-	1.13
13-14	1.50	0.20	-	1.70
15-16	2.00	0.27	-	2.27
17-18	2.50	0.34	-	2.84

* Amount per week spread over a year

The suggested pocket money budget is directly linked to age. Nothing is included for children aged under two years; there is a 20p a week spending allowance for treats for children aged two to four; and 40p a week for those aged five to six. This allowance would buy one packet of sweets or one bar of chocolate a week for pre-school children, and two bars a week for children in the infant classes. Pocket money, it is suggested, rises from 50p a week at age seven to eight, to £2.50 a week at age seventeen to eighteen. It is also suggested that the extra cost of keeping children amused over the summer holidays should be catered for by providing double pocket money over the summer break.

Older teenagers may be able to earn money by baby-sitting, doing paid jobs around the home, or working part-time in local shops. No special allowance has been made for this factor. However, such earnings may help offset some of the clothing and pocket money expenses for older teenagers. The amounts of pocket money allowed for older children may be considered low by current standards.

Modest-but-Adequate Budget Standard
For the Modest-but-Adequate Budget standard the estimate for treats and pocket money is doubled (Table 13.2).

Table 13.2 Weekly Cost of Pocket Money and Treats - Modest-but-Adequate Standard, 1992

Age	Pocket money £	Double pocket money for Summer* £	Sweets £	Total* £
0-2	-	-	-	-
3-4	-	-	0.40	.40
5-6	-	-	0.80	.80
7-8	1.00	0.14	-	1.14
9-10	1.00	0.14	-	1.14
11-12	2.00	0.26	-	2.26
13-14	3.00	0.40	-	3.40
15-16	4.00	0.54	-	4.54
17-18	5.00	0.68	-	5.68

*Amount per week spread over a year.

13.2 Comparison of results

The *Household Budget Survey* shows spending on sweets, ice-cream, and crisps rising with the number of children but, as might be expected, smaller families are likely to spend more per child on such treats (*1987 Household Budget Survey*, 1989, Table 8, codes 179, 180, 188). The *Household Budget Survey* figures for pocket money are relatively low but show consistent growth by age (Table 9, code 430). The global figure for treats and pocket money in the current study is meant to pick up miscellaneous spending on such items as sweets, drinks and comics as well as regular cash handed out in pocket money.

13.3 Summary

- Under the Basic Minimum Budget Standard it is suggested that pocket money is usually paid to children over seven years of age, rising from 50p per week in this age group to £2.50 a week at age seventeen to eighteen. Spending on children aged under seven years is recorded in the study in the form of a spending allowance for treats; 20p a week for two- to four-year-olds; and 40p per week for those aged five to six.
- The allowance for pocket money and treats under the Modest-but-Adequate Budget standard is double the amount allowed under the Basic Minimum Budget standard; £1.00 per week for children aged seven to eight rising to £5.00 per week at age seventeen to eighteen.
- Recorded spending on pocket money will vary from household to household depending on the organisation of spending on treats and pocket money.

Chapter 14 - Outings and Holidays

14. Introduction

Regular outings and occasional holiday breaks should constitute a normal part of youth and adolescence. Figures for the holiday and outings budget (Figure 14.1) assign a notional weekly sum for children of different ages, and allow for more journeys or outings for older children, and for the cost of full fares for children aged over sixteen. No figure is included for the child's share of journeys in the family car. The cost of a holiday is based on the average per capita cost of average bednights away from home as shown in the *Household Budget Survey*, plus an allowance for extra pocket money.

Figure 14.1 below presents the cost of holidays and outings for the two levels of budgets - Basic and Modest-but-Adequate.

Figure 14.1 Weekly Cost of Holidays and Outings, 1992

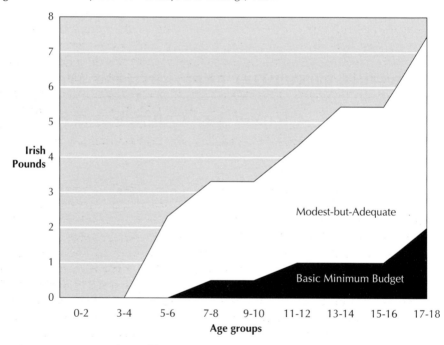

Source: Appendix C, Table C.11

116

14.1 Transport and outings
Basic Minimum Budget Standard and Modest-but-Adequate Budget Standard
Almost two-thirds of all households have a car. This figure is much higher in rural areas where there is limited public transport. The *Household Budget Survey* shows families with children spending £10-£11 a week on petrol, compared to £7 for couples with no children. Families with children may use the car more often, for example for trips to the seaside, or ferrying children to matches. However, the marginal cost of bringing children on a journey which the family would be undertaking anyway is likely to be small. In keeping with the approach of looking at the marginal cost of children, an average weekly figure has been estimated for busfare and outings for the different age groups. Trips connected with school have already been covered under education expenditure.

Children aged under four travel free of charge on the buses; children over sixteen pay full fare. As children become older, they are likely to go out more often, and thus spend more money on transport. A figure of 50p per week is suggested for transport and outings costs for children aged 7-10; £1 a week for children aged eleven to sixteen; and double that for the over sixteens on adult fares. The sums suggested would allow a £2 outing once a month for younger children, and for older children £1 a week, up to age sixteen, and £2 a week for over sixteens on adult fares, which would, for example, pay for a weekly bus trip into central Dublin from the suburbs.

14.2 Holidays
Whether or not the family takes a holiday, summer is an expensive time, with younger children off school for two months, and older children off for up to three months. The *1987 Household Budget Survey*, shows that 30 per cent of households took a holiday away from home (1989, Appendix 6, codes 428 & 235). The urban mothers consulted by the study group reported that school holidays were a particularly expensive time with the need to keep children entertained; extra money was spent on outings to the cinema, on trips to the seaside and on sweets. Few of these families could afford a holiday but some set aside a week of outings/treats for the children over the summer period. The rural mothers consulted were living in a holiday region in the West of Ireland and thus amusement for the children in the summer was found to be much cheaper. Older children, however, would go to discos and other venues that would not be in operation during school term time.

117

Basic Minimum Budget Standard

No holiday spending is shown for children up to four years of age in this study. Their marginal cost as part of a parental holiday would be low and there would be little difference in the cost of keeping them amused in the summer months. In attempting to set a standard for holiday expenditure, the study group took the view that it would be almost as expensive to entertain children by regular outings from home over the whole summer as to take a modest four- to five-day holiday in Ireland. Extra pocket money has been priced for the five-day holiday at £1 a day per child aged from four to eleven. This would, for example, pay for a Coke and an ice cream per day; extra pocket money for older children has been set at £2 a week. It has already been suggested that pocket money would need to be doubled for the remaining weeks of July and August to cover the extra costs of keeping children amused over the summer months. This cost has already been covered under the discussion concerning treats and pocket money.

The *Household Budget Survey* showed an average of 15 person nights holiday per household, or an average of 4.3 nights per person. The average spending per holiday in Ireland worked out at £117 per household, or £38 per head in February 1992 prices (1989, Table 1A, codes 452 & 23). Five pounds pocket money is added in per child from age four to eleven (about £1 a day over the holiday), and £10 pocket money over the holiday for teenagers, which gives an average figure for holiday expenses of 83p a week for primary school children and 92p a week for second level children.

Modest-but-Adequate Budget Standard

To achieve a Modest-but-Adequate Budget Standard a two-week holiday is suggested. The average weekly cost would be £2.32 a week for younger children, and £2.58 for older children. Fares and trips are costed similarly in both the Basic Minimum Budget and the Modest-but-Adequate budget.

The cost of a three-week holiday in the Gaeltacht would amount to £190 per child, plus return trainfare, plus £1 a day pocket money. This total of £225 in all would cost about £4.33 per week spread over that particular year. Allowance has been made in the Modest-but-Adequate Budget standard for one such holiday, costing about 87p a week spread over the five-year second level cycle.

14.3 Summary

- Under the Basic Minimum Budget standard and the Modest-but-Adequate Budget standard expenditure on transport, fares and trips ranges from 50p per week for children aged seven to twelve years to £2.00 per week for thirteen to eighteen year olds.

- One four- to five-day holiday each year is costed at 83p for younger children and 92p for older children under the Basic Minimum Budget.

- A two week holiday annually - including one Gaeltacht holiday for second level students - is costed at £2.32 per week for children aged 7-12 years and £3.45 for 13-18 year olds.

Table A.1 Costings for Dietary Modifications for Boys

Age	1-under 4	4-under 7	7-under 11	11-18
Item	£	£	£	£
Brown bread	0.11	0.20	0.30	0.43
Liver	0.02	0.04	0.04	0.05
Oranges	0.43	0.86	0.86	0.86
Total	0.56	1.10	1.20	1.34

Table A.2 Costings for Dietary Modifications for Girls

Age	1-under 4	4-under 7	7-under 11	11-18
Item	£	£	£	£
Brown bread	0.11	0.20	0.20	0.25
Liver	0.02	0.02	0.04	0.05
Oranges	0.43	0.86	0.86	0.86
Total	0.56	1.08	1.10	1.16

Appendix B

Clothes budgets: Quantity, Lifespan, Price and Weekly Cost

Clothes for under twelves were priced from the medium price range in Dunnes Stores, with T-shirts priced at Penneys. For thirteen to eighteen year olds, the main pricing was done at Penneys, with additional pricing at Dunnes Stores. Shoes were priced at a local shoe shop (Boylan's, Dundrum).

Table B.1 Clothes Budgets for Age 0 - Under 6 Months

Item	Quantity	Lifespan (weeks)	Price £ £	Cost per week
Babygro	6	13	2.95	1.36
Vests	6	13	1.98	0.91
Socks	3	13	0.75	0.17
Booties	2	26	2.50	0.19
Cardigans	4	13	2.99	0.92
Snowsuit	1	26	10.95	0.42
Sleepsuit	2	13	8.95	1.38
Hat	1	26	1.99	0.08
Bibs	6	52	0.50	0.06
Costs				**5.49**
Additional for boys				0.00
Sub-total				0.00
Total cost for a boy				**5.49**
Additional for girls				
Tights	2	13	2.50	0.38
Dresses	2	13	8.95	1.38
Sub-total				1.76
Total cost for a girl				**7.25**

122

Table B.2 Clothes Budgets for Age 6 Months - Under 12 Months

Item	Quantity	Lifespan (weeks)	Price £	Cost per week
Babygrow	3	26	2.95	0.34
Vests	4	26	1.98	0.30
Socks	6	26	0.75	0.17
Booties	2	26	2.50	0.19
Cardigans	2	26	2.99	0.23
Snowsuit	1	26	10.95	0.42
Sleepsuit	2	26	8.95	0.69
Hat/Mittens set	1	26	1.99	0.08
Bibs	6	52	0.50	0.06
Jumpers	2	26	6.95	0.53
Trousers	2	26	7.95	0.61
Polos	3	26	3.00	0.35
Costs				**3.97**
Additional for boys				
Trousers	2	26	7.95	0.61
Sub-total				0.61
Total cost for a boy				**4.58**
Additional for girls				
Tights	2	26	2.50	0.19
Dresses	2	26	8.95	0.69
Sub-total				0.88
Total cost for a girl				**4.85**

Appendix B

Table B.3 Clothes Budgets for Age 1 - 2 Years

Item	Quantity	Lifespan (weeks)	Price £	Cost per week
Vests	4	26	1.98	0.30
Socks	6	26	0.75	0.17
Cardigans	2	26	2.99	0.23
Sleepsuit	2	52	8.95	0.34
Hat/Mittens set	1	52	1.99	0.04
Bibs	6	52	0.50	0.06
Snowsuit	1	52	10.95	0.21
Jumpers	2	26	6.95	0.53
Trousers	2	26	7.95	0.61
Polos	1	52	3.00	0.06
Shoes	1	13	15.00	1.15
Anorak	1	52	14.95	0.29
Pyjamas	2	26	5.50	0.42
Shorts	2	52	1.97	0.08
T-shirts	2	52	2.50	0.10
Underwear	3	26	1.00	0.12
Costs				**4.71**
Additional for boys				
Trousers	2	26	7.95	0.61
Sub-total				0.61
Total costs for a boy				**5.32**
Additional for girls				
Tights	2	26	2.50	0.19
Dresses	2	26	8.95	0.69
Sub-total				0.88
Total costs for a girl				**5.59**

Table B.4 Clothes Budgets for Age 3 - 4 Years

Item	Quantity	Lifespan (weeks)	Price £	Cost per week
Sweater	2	52	6.95	0.27
Shoes	1	26	15.00	0.58
Runners	1	26	5.95	0.23
Vests	2	52	1.75	0.07
Socks	6	26	0.75	0.17
Gloves	1	104	1.99	0.02
Dressing Gown	1	104	9.95	0.10
T-shirts	4	52	5.95	0.46
Anorak	1	52	14.95	0.29
Wellies	1	52	3.95	0.08
Slippers	1	52	4.95	0.10
Shorts	2	52	1.97	0.08
Jeans	1	52	5.00	0.10
Raincoat	1	104	2.95	0.03
Tracksuit	1	52	7.95	0.15
Costs				**2.73**
Additional for boys				
Sweatshirt	1	52	3.99	0.08
Shirts	2	52	2.95	0.11
Pyjamas	2	52	6.95	0.27
Trousers	2	26	6.95	0.53
Underwear	6	26	1.25	0.29
Swimwear	1	104	3.95	0.04
Sub-total				1.32
Total cost for a boy				**4.05**
Additional for girls				
Tights	2	26	2.50	0.19
Dresses	2	26	8.95	0.69
Blouse	2	52	2.95	0.11
Nightgown	2	52	6.95	0.27
Underwear	6	52	1.00	0.12
Swimwear	1	104	3.95	0.04
Sub-total				1.42
Total cost for a girl				**4.15**

Appendix B

Table B.5 Clothes Budgets for Age 5 - 6 Years

Item	Quantity	Lifespan (weeks)	Price £	Cost per week
Sweater	2	52	9.95	0.38
Shoes	1	26	15.00	0.58
Runners	1	26	5.95	0.23
Socks	6	52	1.25	0.14
Vests	2	52	1.75	0.07
Gloves	1	104	1.99	0.02
Dressing Gown	1	104	12.95	0.12
T-shirts	4	52	5.95	0.46
Anorak	1	52	14.95	0.29
Wellies	1	104	3.95	0.04
Scarf	1	156	1.99	0.01
Slippers	1	52	4.95	0.10
Shorts	2	52	3.95	0.15
Jeans	1	52	9.95	0.19
Raincoat	1	104	2.95	0.03
Tracksuit	1	52	7.95	0.15
Costs				**2.96**
Additional for boys				
Sweatshirt	1	52	6.95	0.13
Shirts	2	52	2.95	0.11
Pyjamas	2	52	6.95	0.27
Trousers	3	26	6.95	0.80
Underpants	6	52	1.25	0.14
Swimwear	1	104	3.95	0.04
Sub-total				1.49
Total cost for a boy				**4.45**

Table B.5 is continued opposite

Table B.5 contd Clothes Budgets for Age 5 - 6 Years

Item	Quantity	Lifespan (weeks)	Price £	Cost per week
Additional for girls				
Blouse	2	52	2.95	0.11
Nightgown	2	52	7.95	0.31
Cardigan	1	52	9.95	0.19
Tights	2	52	3.00	0.12
Slips	2	104	2.50	0.05
Underwear	6	52	1.00	0.12
Swimsuit	1	104	6.95	0.07
Shirt	1	52	8.95	0.17
Winter dress	1	52	9.95	0.19
Summer dress	1	52	8.95	0.17
Sub-total				1.50
Total cost for a girl				**4.46**

Appendix B

Table B.6 Clothes Budgets for Age 7 - 12 Years

Item	Quantity	Lifespan (weeks)	Price £	Cost per week
Sweater	2	104	9.95	0.19
Shoes	1	26	20.00	0.77
Runners	1	26	7.95	0.31
Socks	6	52	1.50	0.17
Vests	2	52	1.75	0.07
Gloves	1	52	1.99	0.02
Dressing gown	1	104	12.95	0.12
T-shirts	4	52	5.95	0.46
Anorak	1	52	14.95	0.29
Wellies	1	104	3.95	0.04
Scarf	1	156	1.99	0.01
Slippers	1	52	4.95	0.10
Shorts	2	52	4.95	0.19
Jeans	1	52	12.95	0.25
Raincoat	1	104	2.95	0.03
Tracksuit	1	52	13.95	0.27
Costs				**3.29**
Additional for boys				
Sweatshirt	1	52	6.95	0.13
Shirts	4	52	2.95	0.23
Pyjamas	2	104	6.95	0.13
Trousers	4	26	6.95	1.07
Underpants	6	52	1.25	0.14
Swimwear	1	104	3.95	0.04
Sub-total				1.74
Total cost for a boy				**5.03**

Table B.6 is continued opposite

Table B.6 contd Clothes Budgets for Age 7 - 12 Years

Item	Quantity	Lifespan (weeks)	Price £	Cost per week
Additional for girls				
Blouse	4	52	2.95	0.23
Nightgown	2	52	7.95	0.31
Cardigan	1	104	9.95	0.10
Tights	2	52	3.00	0.12
Slips	2	104	2.50	0.05
Underwear	6	52	1.00	0.12
Swimsuit	1	104	7.95	0.08
Skirt	2	52	8.95	0.34
Winter dress	1	52	9.95	0.19
Summer dress	1	52	15.00	0.29
Sub-total				1.83
Total cost for a girl				**5.12**

Appendix B

Table B.7 Clothes Budgets for Age 13 - 18 Years

Item	Quantity	Lifespan (weeks)	Price £	Cost per week
Shoes	1	26	20.00	0.77
Runners	1	26	20.00	0.77
Socks	6	52	1.75	0.20
Gloves	1	104	5.00	0.05
T-shirts	4	52	6.99	0.54
Anorak	1	104	30.00	0.29
Shorts	2	52	7.99	0.31
Jeans	2	52	16.00	0.62
Docs	1	52	25.00	0.48
Sweatshirt	2	52	9.00	0.35
School jumper	1	52	12.00	0.23
Cost				**4.61**
Additional for Boys				
Sweatshirt	2	104	12.00	0.23
Shirts	4	104	8.99	0.35
Pyjamas	2	104	9.99	0.19
School trousers	2	52	19.00	0.73
Underpants	6	52	1.99	0.23
Swim trunks	1	104	4.99	0.05
Vests	2	52	1.75	0.07
Sub-total				1.85
Total cost for a boy				**6.46**

Table B.7 is continued opposite

Table B.7 contd Clothes Budgets for Age 13 - 18 Years

Item	Quantity	Lifespan (weeks)	Price £	Cost per week
Additional for girls				
Blouses	4	104	9.99	0.38
Nightgown	2	52	9.99	0.38
Cardigan	1	104	17.00	0.16
Leggings	2	104	3.50	0.07
Underwear	9	26	1.99	0.69
Swimsuit	1	104	9.99	0.10
Jumper	1	104	12.00	0.12
Skirts	2	104	14.00	0.27
Bra	3	52	3.99	0.23
Tights	4	8	1.12	0.56
				____
Sub-total				2.69
Total cost for a girl				**7.57**

Appendix C

Figure 1

Table C.1 Weekly Cost of a Child - Basic Minimum Standard, 1992

Age Group/ Item	0-6 £	7-12 £	13-18 £
Food	9.25	14.03	15.95
Clothes	4.80	5.08	7.02
Education	0.49	3.60	4.86
Personal Care	3.07	1.24	2.57
Household Durables	1.33	0.94	0.94
Fuel	0.56	0.56	0.80
Outings/Holidays	0.24	1.50	2.25
Pocket Money/Presents/Toys	0.94	1.53	3.04
Total (rounded to nearest 10p)	**20.70**	**28.50**	**37.40**

Figure 2

Table C.2 Extra Cost for Modest-but-Adequate Standard, 1992

Age Group/ Item	0-6 £	7-12 £	13-18 £
Food	3.08	4.68	5.32
Outings/Holidays	0.43	1.49	2.53
Pocket Money/Presents/Toys	0.49	1.53	3.04
Baby Sitting	1.25	2.50	-
Pre-school	1.04	-	-
Total Extra Costs	**6.74**	**10.20**	**10.89**
Total Costs for Modest-but-Adequate Standard (rounded to nearest 10p)	**27.40**	**36.70**	**48.30**

Appendix C

Figure 2.1

Table C.3 Child Income Support Schemes in Europe, 1991

Country	1st child ECUs	2nd child ECUs	3rd child ECUs	4th & later child ECUs
Belgium	52.0	97.1	145.0	145.0
Denmark	61.8	61.8	61.8	61.8
France	-	87.4	111.8	112.1
Germany	24.4	34.2	68.3	68.3
Greece	4.0	9.9	16.4	27.5
Ireland	20.6	20.6	20.6	29.9
Italy	39.0	39.0	104.0	150.0
Luxembourg	45.7	84.0	177.8	137.6
Netherlands	8.8	8.8	13.3	8.8
Portugal	36.3	52.7	51.7	62.5
Spain	23.4	23.4	23.4	23.4
UK	51.4	45.1	45.1	45.1
Average	**33.4**	**47.0**	**69.9**	**71.9**

Source: European Observatory on National Family Policies, National Family Policies in EC Countries in 1990, EC commission 1991, Table 3 p. 93.
Note: For Belgium and Italy the family allowances for wage-earners have been quoted, rather than for the self-employed. For Greece, the allowances for private sector workers have been taken. In Italy, Greece and Spain, family allowances are means-tested.

Figure 4

Table C.4 Average Weekly Cost of a Child

Commodity Group	Basic Minimum Budget £	Modest-but-Adequate Budget £
Food	12.90	17.20
Clothes	5.60	5.60
Education	2.90	3.40
Personal Care	2.30	4.40
Household Durables	1.10	1.10
Fuel	0.70	0.70
Outings/Holidays	1.30	2.70
Pocket Money/Presents/Toys	1.80	3.60
Baby-sitting	-	1.30
Total	**28.60**	**39.90**

Note 1: All figures are rounded to the nearest 10p
Note 2: The Modest-but-Adequate figure for education includes pre-school education.

Appendix C

Figure 5.2

Table C.5 Average Weekly Food Spending by Family Cycle, 1992

Family Type	Approximate Age Group	Spending £
Pre-school	0 - 4	55.16
Early school	5 - 9	64.21
Pre-adolescent	10 - 14	74.84
Adolescent	15 - 19	83.58

Note: Family cycle is assessed by the age of the eldest child
Source: *1987 Household Budget Survey* (1989), Table 9

Figure 6.1

Table C.6 Weekly Cost of Clothes - Basic Minimum Standard, 1992

Age Group	Boys £	Girls £	Average £
0 - 1	5.04	6.05	5.55
1 - 2	5.32	5.59	5.46
3 - 4	4.05	4.15	4.10
5 - 6	4.45	4.46	4.46
7 - 8	5.03	5.12	5.08
9 - 10	5.03	5.12	5.08
11 - 12	5.03	5.12	5.08
13 - 14	6.46	7.57	7.02
15 - 16	6.46	7.57	7.02
17 - 18	6.46	7.57	7.02

Appendix C

Figure 6.2

Table C. 7 Average Weekly Spending on Children's Clothes by Family size, 1992

Family Type	Weekly Spending £
Couple & 1 child	4.17
Couple & 2 children	5.98
Couple & 3 children	8.25
Couple & 4 children	8.93

Source: *1987 Household Budget Survey,* 1989;
Note: Prices are adjusted by the clothing component of the Consumer Price Index.

Figure 7.1

Table C.8 Educational Costs for Primary and Secondary - Basic Minimum Standard, 1992

Primary School	Age	Annual Cost £	Weekly Cost £
Junior Infants	5	70.34	1.35
Senior Infants	6	106.53	2.05
1st Class	7	145.59	2.80
2nd Class	8	147.52	2.84
3rd Class	9	200.26	3.85
4th Class	10	198.57	3.82
5th Class	11	210.36	4.05
6th Class	12	219.40	4.22

Secondary School	Age	Weekly Cost £	Annual Cost £
1st Year	13	273.42	5.26
2nd Year	14	271.35	5.22
3rd Year	15	306.21	5.89
4th Year	16	310.82	5.98
5th Year	17	353.50	6.80

Appendix C

Figure 8.1

Table C.9 Weekly Cost of Personal Care - Basic Minimum Standard, 1992

Age Group	Boys £	Girls £	Average £
0 - 1	7.64	7.64	7.64
1 - 2	4.43	4.43	4.43
3 - 4	1.24	1.24	1.24
5 - 6	1.24	1.24	1.24
7 - 8	1.24	1.24	1.24
9 - 10	1.24	1.24	1.24
11 - 12	1.24	1.24	1.24
13 - 14	2.39	2.71	2.55
15 - 16	2.39	2.71	2.55
17 - 18	2.52	2.71	2.62

Figure 9.1

Table C.10 Housing Costs by Tenure, 1987

Tenure	Percentage of expenditure %	Percentage of households %
Owned outright	4.0	41.0
Owned with mortgage	12.3	35.0
Local Authority	6.7	14.0
Private rented	14.3	8.0

Source: *1987 Household Budget Survey*, Table 4, 1989.

Appendix C

Figure 14.1

Table C.11 Weekly Cost of Holidays and Outings per year - Basic Minimum Standard and Modest-but-Adequate Standard, 1992

Age	Basic Minimum Budget			Modest-but-Adequate			
	Fares/ trips £	Holiday £	Total £	Fares/ trips £	Holiday £	Gaeltacht £	Total £
0-2	-	-	-	-	-	-	-
3-4	-	-	-	-	-	-	-
5-6	-	0.83	0.83	-	2.32	-	2.32
7-8	0.50	0.83	1.33	0.50	2.32	-	2.82
9-10	0.50	0.83	1.33	0.50	2.32	-	2.82
11-12	1.00	0.83	1.83	1.00	2.32	-	3.32
13-14	1.00	0.92	1.92	1.00	2.58	0.87	4.45
15-16	1.00	0.92	1.92	1.00	2.58	0.87	4.45
17-18	2.00	0.92	2.92	2.00	2.58	0.87	5.45

Bibliography

Adler, M and S Asquith (1981) *Discretion and Welfare,* Heinemann, London.

Baldwin, S and C Godfrey (1983) *Economies of Scale in Large, Low-income Families* (mimeo), University of York, Social Policy Research Unit.

Bradshaw, J (ed.)(1993) *Budget Standards for the United Kingdom,* Studies in Cash and Care series, Avebury, Hants.

Bradshaw, J and J Ernst (1990) *Establishing a Modest but Adequate Budget for a British Family,* University of York: Family Budget Unit, Working Paper No. 2.

Bradshaw, J and J Morgan (1987) *Budgeting on Benefit: The Consumption of Families on Social Security,* Family Policy Studies Centre, UK.

Bradshaw, J, D Mitchell and J Morgan (1987), 'Evaluating Adequacy: The Potential of Budget Standards', *Journal of Social Policy,* Vol. 16(2), 167-181.

Brown, J(1988) *Child Benefit: Investing in the Future,* Child Poverty Action Group, London.

Callan, T (1991) *Income Tax and Welfare Reforms: Microsimulation Modelling and Analysis,* Economic and Social Research Institute, ESRI General Research Series, Paper No. 154.

Callan, T, B Nolan, B J Whelan, DF Hannan with S Creighton (1989) *Poverty, Income and Welfare in Ireland,* Economic and Social Research Institute, ESRI General Research Series Paper No. 146.

Callan, T, DF Hannan, B Nolan, B J Whelan and S Creighton (1988) *Poverty and the Social Welfare System in Ireland,* Combat Poverty Agency, Research Report Series, Dublin.

Carmichael, K (1981) 'The Path of the Delinquent' in G Cook and V Richardson (eds) *Juvenile Justice at the Crossroads,* Family Studies Centre, University College Dublin.

Carney, C (1985) 'Access to School Meals: the Constraints of Permissive Legislation', *The Irish Journal of Education,* Vol. 19, 1,2.

Carney, C (1986) 'Free School Books, A Re-Distributive Failure?' *Administration,* Vol. 34(3).

Carney, C (1991) *Selectivity Issues in Irish Social Services,* Family Studies Centre, University College Dublin.

Central Statistics Office (1989) *Household Budget Survey* 1987, Vols. 1 and 2, Dublin.

Claude, M and M Moutardier (November 1991) 'Une Évaluation du coût Direct de l'enfant de 1979 à 1989', *Economie et Statistique,* No.248.

143

Bibliography

Commission on Social Welfare (1986) *Report of the Commission on Social Welfare,* Government Publications, Dublin.

Conference of Major Religious Superiors (1993) *New Frontiers for Full Citizenship,* Dublin

Conniffe, D and G Keogh (1988) *Equivalence Scales and Costs of Children,* Economic and Social Research Institute, ESRI General Research Series Paper No. 142.

Cooke, K and S Baldwin (1984) *How Much is Enough? A Review of Supplementary Benefit Scale Rates,* Family Policy Studies Centre, Occasional Paper No. 1, UK.

Deacon, B and J Bradshaw (1983) *Reserved for the Poor,* Martin Robertson, London.

de Hoog, K and J van Ophem (1991) *Poor Families in the Netherlands: Strategies of Nuclear and One Parent Families,* Department of Household and Consumer Studies, University of Wageningen, Netherlands.

Department of Social Welfare (1990 & 1991a) *Statistical Information on Social Welfare Services,* Government Publications, Dublin.

Department of Social Welfare (1991b) *Report of the Review Group on the Treatment of Households in the Social Welfare Code,* Department of Social Welfare, Dublin.

Department of Social Welfare (1992) *Rates of Payment,* Department of Social Welfare, Dublin.

Department of Social Welfare (1993) *Rates of Payment,* Department of Social Welfare, Dublin.

European Observatory on Family Policies (1991) *Families and Policies: Evolution and Trends in 1989-90,* Commission of the European Communities.

Family Budget Unit (1990) *The Work of the Family Budget Unit,* University of York; working papers 1-13 dealing with different commodity groups.

Gormley, T R, T Walshe, K Cormican (1989) *Assessment of School Meals and of Growth, Food Intake and Food Likes/Dislikes of Primary School Children in Inner City Dublin Schools,* Combat Poverty Agency Research Report Series No.1., Dublin.

Henwood, M and M Wicks (1986) *Benefit or Burden? The Objectives and Impact of Child Support,* Family Policy Studies Centre, UK.

Joshi, H (1987) *The Cash Opportunity Costs of Childbearing: An Approach to Estimation using British Data,* Centre for Economic Policy Research, Paper 208.

Joshi, H (1987) 'The Cost of Caring' in C. Glendinning and J. Millar (eds) *Women and Poverty in Britain,* Wheatsheaf Books, Brighton.

Joshi, H and S Owen (1983) *How Many Pensionable Years? The Lifetime Earning History of Men and Women*, London DHSS, Economic Advisers' Office.

Kennedy, F (1989) *Family Economy and Government in Ireland*, Economic and Social Research Institute, ESRI General Research Series Paper No. 143.

Kennedy Report (1970) *Report on the Reformatory and Industrial Schools Systems*, Government Publications, Dublin.

Lamale, M and M S Stolz (1960) 'The Interim City Worker's Family Budget', *US. Monthly Labor Review*, Vol. 83(8), 785-808.

Lee, P and M Gibney (1989) *Patterns of Food and Nutrient Intake in a Suburb of Dublin with Chronically High Unemployment*, Combat Poverty Agency Research Report Series No. 2., Dublin.

Lynes, T (1979) 'Costs of Children', *New Society*, 15 November, 1979.

McClements, L (1978) *The Economics of Social Security*, Heinemann, London.

McGee, H and M Fitzgerald (1988) *Pathways to Child Hospitalization*, Health Promotion Unit, Department of Health.

Mack, J and S Lansley (1985) *Poor Britain*, George Allen, London.

Miller, J, S Leeper and C Davies (1992) *Lone Parents: Poverty and Public Policy in Ireland*, Combat Poverty Agency Research Report Series No. 15, Dublin

Mitchell, D A (1985) *Constructing a Poverty Line for the UK: an Exploration of the Budget Standard Approach*, Unpublished MA Dissertation, University of York.

Mitchell, D A and K Cooke (1988) 'The Cost of Child Rearing' in R. Walker and G. Parker (eds), *Money Matters: Income, Wealth and Welfare*, Sage, London.

Mollan, C (1983) 'Families and Children: A Discussion Document About Families and Family Support', CARE, Dublin.

Muellbauer, J (1980) 'The Estimation of the Prais-Houthakker Model of Equivalence Scales', *Econometrica*.

Murphy-Lawless, J (1990) *A Working Bibliography on Data Related to Child Poverty in Ireland: a Report for the Combat Poverty Agency*, Unpublished, Combat Poverty Agency, Dublin.

Murphy-Lawless, J (1992) T*he Adequacy of Income and Family Expenditure*, Combat Poverty Agency Research Report Series No. 14, Dublin.

Bibliography

National Parents Council - Primary (1990) *The Cost of Free Education: A Survey on the Costs to Parents of Free Primary Education in Ireland*, Government Publications, Dublin.

National Parents Council - Post-Primary (1991) *Textbooks, What a Price*, Department of Education, Dublin.

New York Community Council (NYCC) (1982) *A Family Budget Standard*, NYCC Budget Standard Service, New York.

Nolan, B (1993) Reforming Child Income Support, *Poverty and Policy 1*, Combat Poverty Agency Policy Document, Dublin

Nolan, B and B Farrell (1990) *Child Poverty in Ireland*, Combat Poverty Agency Research Report Series No.7., Dublin.

O'Brien, M and A O'Hare (1992) *Treated Drug Misuse in the Greater Dublin Area 1990*, Health Research Board, Dublin.

Oldfield, N and A C S Yu (1993) *The Cost of A Child: Living Standards for the 1990s*, Child Poverty Action Group, London.

Oppenheim, C (1988) *The Cost of a Child*, Child Poverty Action Group, London.

Optalic Department, College of Technology, Kevin Street, Dublin, *Personal Contact*.

Page, R (1984) *Stigma*, Routledge and Kegan Paul, London.

Parker, H (1978) *Who Pays for the Children: A New Approach to Family Income Support*, The Outer Circle Poverty Unit, London.

PAUL Project, (1991) *Educational Costs and Welfare Provisions for Low-income Families*, Limerick.

Piachaud, D (1979) *The Cost of a Child*, Child Poverty Pamphlet No. 43, London.

Piachaud, D (1981) *Children and Poverty*, Child Poverty Action Group, London.

Piachaud, D (1984) *Round About Fifty Hours a Week: the Time Costs of Children*, Child Poverty Action Group, London.

Purchase, Berning, and Lyng (1982) 'The Cost of Washing Clothes - Sources of Variation', *Journal of Consumer Studies and Home Economics*

Roll, J (1986) *Babies and Money: Birth Trends and Costs*, Family Policy Studies Centre, UK.

Rottman, D B (1985) *The Criminal Justice System: Policy and Performance*, National

Bibliography

Economic and Social Council, Paper No.77. Government Publications, Dublin.

Rowntree, B S (1901) *Poverty: A Study of Town Life*, Macmillan, London.

Rowntree, B S (1937) *The Human Needs of Labour*, Longmans, London.

Rowntree, B.S (1941) *Poverty and Progress*, Longmans, London.

Select Committee on Crime (1992) *Juvenile Crime: Its causes and its remedies*, (First Report of the Select Committee on Crime), Government Publications, Dublin.

Social Planning Council (1981) T*he Budgets Guide Methodology Study*, Toronto.

Society of St. Vincent de Paul (1986) *Submission to the Comission on Social Welfare*, Dublin.

Spicker, P (1984) *Stigma and Social Welfare*, Croom Helm, Kent.

Sitt, S and D Grant (1993) *Poverty: Rowntree Revisited*, Liverpool John Moores University, Avebury, Hants.

Stitt, S (1989) *Poverty, Incomes and Supplementary Benefits: A Test of Adequacy by Segregation*, Unpublished Ph.D. Thesis, Queens University, Belfast.

Swedish National Board for Consumer Policies (1989) *Calculation of Consumer Costs*, Sweden.

Townsend, P (1979) *Poverty in the United Kingdom*, Penguin, Harmondsworth.

U S Bureau of Labor Statistics (1948) *A Workers Budget in the United States*, Bulletin No. 927, Washington DC.

Watts, H (1980) *New American Family Budget Standards Report by the Expert Committee on Family Budget Revisions*, Institute for Research on Poverty, University of Wisconsin.

Williams, J and Whelan, B (1985) *Report on Survey of St. Vincent de Paul Conferences*, Economic and Social Research Institute, Dublin.

Wynn, M (1970) *Family Policy*, Michael Joseph, London.

Combat Poverty Agency Publications

Research Report Series

No. 1   T.R. GORMLEY et al (1989); Assessment of School Meals and Growth, Food Intake and Food Likes/Dislikes of Primary School Children in Inner City Dublin Schools; £2.00.

No. 2   P. LEE and M. GIBNEY (1989); Patterns of Food and Nutrient Intake in a Suburb of Dublin with Chronically High Unemployment; £2.00.

No. 3   B. DILLON (1989); A Review and Recent History of the Coolock Community Law Centre; £2.00.

No. 4   B. CULLEN(1989); Poverty, Community and Development; £3.00.

No. 5   S. BYRNE (1990); Wealth and the Wealthy in Ireland; £2.00.

No. 6   P. WARD (1990); Financial Consequences of Marital Breakdown; £4.00.

No. 7   B. NOLAN and B. FARRELL (1990); Child Poverty in Ireland; £4.00.

No. 8   L. HAYES (1990); Working for Change, A Study of Three Women's Community Projects; £4.00.

No. 9   D. DONNISON et al (1991); Urban Poverty, the Economy and Public Policy; £5.00.

No. 10   F. MILLS et al (1991); Scheme of Last Resort?: a review of Supplementary Welfare Allowance; £6.00.

No. 11   C. MULVEY (1991); Report on the Department of Social Welfare's Grants Scheme for Locally based Women's Groups; £2.00.

No.12   B. NOLAN (1991); The Wealth of Irish Households; £6.00.

No. 13   P. KELLEHER and M. WHELAN (1992); Dublin Communities in Action; A Study of Six Projects; (with Community Action Network); £6.00.

No. 14   J. MURPHY LAWLESS (1992); The Adequacy of Income and Family Expenditure; £6.00.

No. 15   J. MILLAR, S. LEEPER, C. DAVIES (1992); Lone Parents, Poverty and Public Policy in Ireland; £6.00.

No. 16   J. WILLIAMS and B. WHELAN, (1994); The Dynamics of Poverty; £6.00.

No. 17   C. CARNEY et al (1994); The Cost of a Child; £6.00.

Recent Policy Documents

Towards a Policy for Combating Poverty among Women (1990); £3.00.

Poverty - An Agenda for the '90s (1989), Free.

Tackling Poverty in the Nineties (1990), Free.

Making Social Rights a Reality (1991), Free.

Building a Fairer Future (1992), Free

Education, Inequality and Poverty (1993), Free

A Programme for Social Equity (1993), Free

A Budget for Social Inclusion (1993), Free

Poverty & Policy 1, B. Nolan (1993); Reforming Child Income Support; £1.00.

A complete list of Agency publications, including resource materials, conference reports and policy statements, is available from the Agency at 8 Charlemont Street, Dublin 2.